A RATHER BUMPY
LIFE PILGRIMAGE

mine and ours

Susan Sayers

Brimstone Press

ACKNOWLEDGEMENTS

I would like to express my deep thanks to all those who have accompanied me on the journey so far, some of whom I have mentioned by name but many more I have not mentioned, but whose love, forgiveness and encouragement I so much value.

Thank you!

Many thanks too to those who have helped to make this publication possible, without whose practical and technical skills, and calm understanding I would have given up. The reader, Philip Painter, and the amazing Brimstone Press leave me speechless with admiration.

Thank you!

ISBN: 978 1906 38591 0

First Published by the author, through Brimstone Press

www.brimstone-press.com

CONTENTS

WHY DID I WRITE THIS BOOK?

OUR BUMPY JOURNEYS OF FAITH

In September 2020 I made a week's pilgrimage of Thanksgiving for Life.

Having just recovered from another stroke, and Covid, I felt an urgent longing to do this, and as it happened, I unknowingly chose the small window of opportunity between the first and second wave of the virus. It wasn't only that I was thankful to be still alive, although of course that thankfulness was huge. It was also that the whole experience of 2020 was making many of us marvel with fresh wonder at the gift and privilege of Life itself.

As I walked the 62 miles from my home church of St Alban's Westcliff, in Southend-on-Sea, to the city of St Alban's in Hertfordshire, with the help of my off-road walker, the ordnance survey app on my phone, and such kindness and hospitality along the way, I began to understand more about the way our whole life is pilgrimage.

So that's why I am writing this book. All it does is trace one person's (my) life pilgrimage as the contorted and muddled journey of faith it has been and is. Of course it can only be the story as I have seen and experienced it, and I'm well aware that others will have very different perceptions and memories. Now that I'm seventy six I can't be bothered any more with editing or selecting events to reveal a person I'd like to be but know I'm not. Instead, I'm attempting to be honest, and I'm pretty certain there will be those who remember things differently. I'm pretty certain I have remembered some things wrong; that some events I have become so used to editing in my favour that it's difficult to discern what really happened.

So I need to ask for your patience, tolerance and understanding as you read. And I hope that this account of my life pilgrimage might help you on yours. Really a journey of anyone's faith is not actually about them, any more than mine is about me. It is the story of how Jesus searches for us when we are lost, and carries us home.

This faith journey story ends with the memories of my week's pilgrimage to St Alban's, and perhaps, if you have managed to read that far, you will better understand what I myself found: that a walking pilgrimage is like a parable, or model, of that unique journey of faith each one of us makes, from birth to death. All of it is holy, I suspect, as far as God is concerned!

CHAPTER 1

BEGINNINGS

As I start this account I am immediately floundering.

After all, my own entry into life was certainly not a true beginning. It was only possible because of my parents and all those in my ancestry whose genes I share, right back to the first life on this planet, and further back, still, to the unknown dying stars, the dust from which our solar system formed. Further back, still, to the beginning of the universe itself. Back, some would say, to the great Creator, though many would disagree with that, including me in my twenties!

But as this is the record of a personal pilgrimage, a journey of faith, and since we can all run our minds back over the aeons of time and development which brought us to our own birth, I would like to start with my parents. They, after all, are a very important part of my pilgrimage, and I'd like you to meet them.

My mother was born in October 1912, and named Audrey Ethel. She loathed her second name, bequeathed to her in honour of her mother, Ethel Maud. She loathed it so much that my sister and I were not given middle names in case we also loathed them, although she did tell me once that she would have given us both the middle name of Mary if we'd been given one at all. I did much later have a three year old friend who felt sorry for me not having one, and as he was passionately into lawn mowers at the time, he gave me the middle name of Flymo. I've thought of this as my very special middle name ever since.

My parents, Audrey and Gordon, on their wedding day.

Audrey's family came from London, and one of her three older brothers, Harold, was a sickly child. The doctor advised the family to move out of the smogs of London to Southend so that Harold could benefit from the clean sea air, and play in the healthy mud.

So down the family came, presumably on the newly opened railway, where little Audrey was born soon after, and her sister

Mabel after her. Mabel couldn't pronounce her own name so called herself Min, a name which stayed with her throughout her life. The sickly Harold thrived, playing in the mud. He ended up sailing the world as a marine engineer, settling finally in Guernsey where he married Ada and they had three sons. At one time anyone on Guernsey with my Mum's surname was probably related to me!

One of the things my Mum talked about was the way her mother had made no secret of the fact that she'd tried her best to end her pregnancy when she found she was expecting Audrey. She already had three growing boys and not much money, so it's very understandable. But I sometimes wonder if this had anything to do with Mum's tough resilience and formidable determination! She remembered herself as quite a rough child, which wasn't surprising with three older brothers. One of them – Leslie – made friends with a boy whose family had recently moved to Southend from West Ham. This friend, Gordon, now lived near the Morris family, and the two boys would run behind Audrey when she was five, and had had a mole on her nose removed. They'd call out, "You got a bit of puddin' on yer nose!" Audrey was always a fast runner though.

When she started school they asked her name. She thought it was Sue Gilroy rather than Audrey Morris. This was because the rest of the family called her 'sister Sue', and their Dad's stage name was Arthur Gilroy. He was a professional whistler, or 'souffleur', as he described himself. The family were often given tickets to watch him from the gods (the highest seats) in the days of music hall entertainment. Wearing evening dress, his specialty was describing a walk in the countryside, making all the different birdsongs. Their Dad would also pick up on acrobatics and magic tricks from fellow performers and pass these skills on to the children. He was a gambler, so money was often scarce, and the family seem to have moved around quite often to avoid the bailiffs. Mum's favourite artist was Lowry and when I went to an exhibition of Lowry's paintings recently, I found one picture of the bailiffs carrying out the furniture, something Mum had graphically described. No wonder she liked his art – it mirrored her own early life.

She and her sister were 'mortified' when an anonymous well wisher had noticed they were short of food and they were to have a free daily lunch at a café. They had little else, but they still had their pride! She and my Auntie Min later used to sometimes burst into a singsong memory of a waitress at this café, and I can still remember it now:

"Roast beef, pie, dinner, ducks, ah ha!"

They'd end their full volume recitation in gusts of laughter.

After winning a scholarship to the local Convent School of St Bernard's, there wasn't money enough for uniform, but once again I gather well wishers helped out. Various lodgers were squashed into the house to eke out the finances and their Mum took in washing which dried and steamed in front of the fire. But she had no idea of how to cook cheap and nutritious food, so when Mum eventually worked in the city at an insurance firm (she wasn't able to stay on at school after Matric as they needed her to have an income) she and her friend Alice enrolled on a smart cookery course during her lunch break. Whenever she was cooking or teaching us to cook, she always kept to the principles she had learnt. "Have ready..." she'd say in her teacher's posh voice, as we got everything out before we started to bake. I still do it now!

So eventually she married her brother Leslie's friend Gordon.

Gordon, who was born in Murchison Road, just off Leyton Highroad, in January 1910, was an only child with parents who had financial security, and, unlike the Morris family, rarely needed to move house. In fact they owned their home, rather than renting. I imagine Gordon spent plenty of time in the rather crazy, noisy, but mainly happy household of his friend.

In Leyton he'd often explored the lakes and woods opposite Whipps Cross hospital. He used to collect wild mushrooms and shoot rabbits with his father, and once floated his boots down the River Pant at Braintree, to see if they got to Southend, where his grandparents lived. That episode earned him the strap, as did many other experiments. At school my Dad would quite often be sent to get the cane across the palms of the hands. Cunningly he sometimes managed to sneak to the cold washrooms where he'd rub his hands along the sinks to make red lines before returning to the classroom. The teacher, seeing the lines, would be satisfied, and he avoided both the pain and the humiliation. Gordon also regularly played truant. Once he and his friend hid in some pipes which started rolling downhill so they had to escape.

Yet he went to the Southend High School for Boys, and loved poetry, became a scout leader and an officer in the TA so was in active service in WW2 in Norway, returning on the same ship as the Norwegian king, from Tromso. Next he was stationed in Gibraltar and then Italy. He was always funny and made people laugh. At heart he was an artist, both with paints and photography. Part of his army work was in Intelligence, analysing 3D aerial photographs, so in Gibraltar they created a darkroom which I gather was often in use, both officially and unofficially.

When they were children both my parents went to church. This involved attendance at the packed Sunday School, where my Mum's oldest brother Eddie had a silver topped cane and kept the children in order. My Mum always got fits of the giggles in church, I remember, so I imagine she did then too, especially as this smart young man was her brother!

Her Mum would march the children round to different churches for evening service, just to see what they were like, and one Sunday they came home excited by a church in Leigh-on-Sea called St Clements, where the ministers wore little hats, there were candles, bells, clouds of incense and oh my word they were very taken with it! After that the whole family shifted to St Clements. I think they found it mysterious, awesome and quite theatrical, which of course they loved.

It was here at St Clements that their real relationship with God developed. At that time Canon King was rector. His uncle was the well loved bishop of Lincoln, and they were taught well. The curate at that time, Harry Greaves, was a young family man from Burton upon Trent, who had fought in WW1, been taken prisoner and escaped, been shot through the face and survived, lost his faith through the trenches horror, and been helped through this by the army padre. Once demobbed he trained for ordination, and St Clements was his first curacy.

He would lead the evening congregation outside and preach on street corners as a soldier priest to the passers by. Crowds would stop to listen, then join the procession back into church, where God was worshipped and adored, and spiritual wounds were tended and healed. God's love, earthed in our mess, resonated with those who had lived and suffered through WW1. My parents remembered the church being so full that people were sitting on the pulpit steps, and standing at the back. Many responded to this priest's shared experience of the recent terrible war, hearing how his faith had also been shaken but subsequently strengthened. Certainly many were helped in their own faith journey, including my parents.

Gordon soon applied to be a server and was told there were no vacancies as they had so many people there. Eventually he was offered a place, and became a tall, upright and reliable thurifer who swung the censor of incense. I imagine the necessary fire lighting was also attractive – my Dad always loved building and stoking fires! Gordon and Audrey were married at St Clements. Audrey designed her gown and her clever dressmaking sister Min made it for her. It was rich brown velvet with gold trimmings, gold veil and gold shoes. She carried gold coloured flowers. She chose this dramatic though unusual colour scheme because they couldn't afford top hat and tails for Gordon, so she didn't want to wear white. But I think they must both have looked wonderful.

They rented a house in Rochford, not far from Southend, and Audrey had to give up her city job when she got married. She was so bored one day that she ate a whole packet of custard creams. Gordon would wave his white hanky out of the train window which was her signal to start cooking the vegetables so that food was ready and waiting as Gordon walked in. They were both excellent darts players and would walk through Rochford playing darts and winning drinks at every pub before rolling home.

Soon their first baby was born. His name was John. Sadly he died soon after his birth so I never met my big brother. But his birthday was always remembered, and he was part of the family. Mum used to say he just looked asleep, and the staff dressed him in his white nightie with a lily in his hands. She never forgot him. I don't remember Dad ever talking about him. They bound Mum's breasts, but of course the milk poured out anyway. My Dad took her on holiday to Devon. He also bought her a book to cheer her up, with the rather unfortunate title, *Gone with the Wind*.

War was brewing. It must have been a grim time for them. Soon Gordon was away fighting. There were times of leave, though, and as Gordon was now an officer, their next child, Margaret, was born at a posh but rather officious Officers' Nursing Home in 1943.

Finally the war ended. Along with many others, my Dad came home in the new year of 1946, so that in September, when the great bulge of babies arrived, including me, there were no midwives to be had. Happily Mollie, a young midwife in training at the London hospital, had been billeted with my Mum, so she became my midwife and godmother. A natural, easy birth at home. I was baptised soon after, so that Mollie could be there before she returned to London. My other godparents were Marjorie and Leslie Curtois, whose son, my 'godbrother' Brian Curtois eventually became a household name as the BBC political correspondent.

And that was my beginning.

CHAPTER 2

EARLY YEARS

The house where I was born was in St David's Drive in Leigh-on-Sea, near Southend. It was a semi-detached house my Mum had bought during the war, when houses were cheaper, and we lived there till I was one.

That first year of my life the winter was very cold, with lots of ice and accumulating snow, so apparently I would be put to bed during the day by an open window as I couldn't be taken out in the pram for most of the winter. I didn't think I remembered anything of this time, but many years later, when I was in my forties, I was asked to babysit and recognised the address. I was shocked to find how familiar the tiles round the fireplace were, and asked my Mum if I could really have remembered them. "Oh well," she said, "because we couldn't go out much that year we spent most of the time in the room with that fireplace!"

Dad's parents had bought a sizeable plot of land near the new Southend hospital, and Grandad designed and planted up the garden so it would be in place once the house was built. They called it Stondon Lodge after the village in Essex which Dad's mother had known and loved as she was growing up. Our family was soon to move into Stondon Lodge with my Dad's parents.

I never did know why. Maybe selling the Leigh house would have enabled him to buy his boat – *Mouette*. Maybe as an army officer he preferred the idea of living in a large detached house. Maybe he was more affected by the war than was realised. Whatever the reason, moving day was to be the day after my first birthday, so I could still have my birthday at the Leigh house.

I presume this reflects something of my Mum's and sister's sadness at leaving. Certainly my sister remembers that house with great affection.

It must have been during this time of living as one extended family that I grew to love my Dad's mother, Florence. We knew her as Nanna Orme, and to my Mum she was Mum Orme. I can remember lying back on her lap on the soft flowery dress she wore, and somehow I knew she loved me. She worshipped at a Congregational church, and ran tea and cake fund-raisers in a white canvas marquee that Grandad and Dad would put up in the garden.

Ten months later everything changed. One day that summer Nanna Orme, who was diabetic, went on a church outing to Worthing for the day, and died there. Soon after, Grandad remarried, and in preparation Stondon Lodge became two flats. Grandad and Auntie Edith were to live downstairs and my family upstairs. The stairs had led round into the hallway, but now the lower section was cut out and rebuilt to end at the front door, so the two flats could be more separated. I remember being swung over what seemed like a huge black chasm while the alterations were made. A bath top was fixed to the bathroom wall, and a sink replaced the wash basin, so this room became both our bathroom and kitchen. The main bedroom became our living room. These alterations must have happened quickly because Nanna died in August, and Grandad's marriage took place in the autumn. The flats had to be ready. I presume Grandad and Edith had already been together for quite a while, but I don't know whether Nanna knew about this or not.

From now on the dark downstairs was totally off limits to us. I suppose our growing family was probably now in the way. I don't think anything legal was drawn up, but certainly all through my childhood we all knew that if Grandad died first we would be on the street. My Mum was pregnant through these changes, and my brother David was born in February 1949.

I liked living upstairs, on a level with the birds. The garden had been divided as well as the house, and we were allowed in the front and side garden. In the long back garden we were allowed to hang out washing, but apart from this it was strictly out of bounds, as too was the garage.

I found the garage irresistible. It smelt of apples, Grandad's soldier greatcoat and helmet hung up like a ghost, a knife grinder made a wonderful whirring if you wound it up, and there was so much to look at and explore behind my Dad's huge bicycle. Often, absorbed in my exploration, I would jump out of my skin as Grandad silently and suddenly appeared, angrily shouting, "What do you think you're doing in here!?" I bolted. Grandad had become a frightening enemy.

When Nanna had been alive, I think Grandad and I were friends. I would help him pick apples, put ice cream into the buried sink under the back garden to keep it cool, and get in the way while he and Dad erected the big white marquee to dry off if it had been put away wet. Now I was glad we lived in the light upstairs and only saw Grandad slinking like a shadow down the hall. It must have been harder for my big sister Margaret, though, as she was three years older.

I'm sure there were reasons for Grandad's changed behaviour. Maybe there was unhealed guilt, or embarrassment. Maybe Auntie Edith had insisted on this clear separation. And I think the whisky had something to do with it, too. Grandad had a dicky heart apparently, and that's why he stopped going out, and became a heavy drinker. I know I didn't dislike him, I was just scared of him. My intense dislike was reserved for his new wife! There was one occasion when she was to babysit us. I screamed non-stop and made it as clear to her as I could that she had no business to be looking after me. She never babysat us again, poor woman!

I was now middle child and two and a half years old. We lived perched up in our upstairs flat until I was twenty. Dad would smile and wave his serviette when passers by looked up curiously at us sitting round our dining table in a bedroom! But of course this room was now our living room, with a bookcase Dad had cleverly doctored to mask the washbasin. I shared a bedroom with Margaret, who very kindly used to write a bedtime story for me every night. I'm sorry to say I'd usually fallen asleep before she finished writing and reading it to me. We used to play a game where one of us got into a weird position in bed, and the other one had to work out what that position was.

Margaret was tidy and I certainly wasn't, so there was an invisible line down the middle of our room. The wash basin froze in the winter, and the windows iced up on the inside. I remember warming a penny in bed before pressing it to the window to make a peephole through the ice. On summer evenings we'd wave to the next door neighbour as he watered his garden, and try to giggle quietly when he aimed the hose at us for fun. He was a professional gardener and it showed. His wife was mentally ill and eventually lived in a mental hospital. I once dressed a small doll as an angel and gave it to her. I remember her being surprised and amused that it was a black doll. I hadn't noticed.

Faith is often laid down very early, as our trust in those who love us prepares the ground for trust in a loving God. I felt greatly blessed to have been born postwar. This meant that our Dads didn't disappear for months at a time, as had been the case for my sister and her contemporaries. Also, I had avoided those scary stories of the frequent bombing and loss which were still being clearly remembered and talked about. Wherever I went I saw gaps among houses, with wallpaper hanging off like ghosts of a family's life. Among the ruined lives were growing rosebay willow-herb, cow parsley and dandelions. I thought it lovely that God was kindly changing these horrible wounds into gardens. I think at this time I linked God and Nature together.

In spite of all the hardships in these postwar years, there was a collective sense of relief. I was one of the many new lives that symbolised the new life and hope of the adults, and my parents' love for me was not ambitious or possessive, but relaxed and thankful. Both were more inclined to laugh and enjoy life than grumble. At school the teachers cheerfully crammed us all into the classrooms, taught us racy folk songs which I'm sure I didn't understand at the time, and treated us to all the new educational aids and modern thinking. We were the first ones of a new age; the NHS is as old as I am, and it was a privilege to be young, alive, and not at war. For me it was a good ground to grow in. I was often told just to do my best, which I took to mean I didn't need to push myself too hard!

Both Mum and Dad were exciting parents to have, which suited me well. Mum refused to teach me to read before school, but was happy to teach me to bake cakes and make surprise dinners from leftovers, to build sea walls from sand till the incoming tide won, and to play catch in the park. Dad always experimented with his cooking, and everything else, putting food colouring in our hot milk for fun, serving Weetabix spread with butter and jam, or tomatoes with tops sliced off and sugar sprinkled on them, served in an egg cup with a teaspoon to scoop the fruit out. His curries would have all kinds of ingredients added, and he often added a spoon of marmalade to his bacon.

I would watch Dad painting, using his black metal box of watercolours, and 1 learnt a lot, fascinated by all the different colours he could make by mixing.

I also lost all sense of time in painting. The family had a saying: "Susan wanted to paint. So she painted!" I would even refuse to eat apparently, if I was painting.

His pen and ink, or pencil drawings were sharp and precise, but the landscapes he painted without any preliminary drawing. He worked fast, until suddenly the blotches of paint would resolve into a focused place I felt I could walk into. And the paint box colours were a mess. Cleaning them and the brushes seemed to be part of this absorbing activity.

While Mum was a town person who loved the sea and walked us down to the beach and mud every day in the holidays, Dad loved the countryside, took us for long walks, showed us how to read and trust maps, and could make whistles from elder or cow parsley. He often teased us, and we were always being tricked… I remember giggling when I'd suddenly find Dad walking in time with my short fast steps. Or David and I would be walking on either side of Dad, holding his hand, and suddenly realise he had joined our hands together and he was grinning as he walked behind us. I remember Mum and I, helpless with laughter as we sat on a draughty train station and Mum made her old green coat into different shapes so she wouldn't need to buy a new one. I remember when I was a Brownie standing at one end of a snowy field while Dad, in army khaki, stood at the far end, as we semaphored messages to each other.

In all this their own faith shone through. This faith was their obvious sense of knowing themselves accepted, forgiven and loved; freedom and joy rather than rules and guilt. I picked up on God's abundant love through theirs. And right from the start I knew God as my friend who was also the loving, creative maker. Three growing children in an upstairs flat could be noisy for those living below, so we spent a huge amount of time outside. Then when we got home and climbed the stairs it was time for drawing, reading, building with bricks or playing trains. We were as quiet as possible. None of us wanted to start Grandad's rage. So I think from early on in my life I sensed the loving God, not only through people, but through the wonder and beauty of nature. The natural world was my playground every day, and it felt to me like God: a very big, very beautiful friend. I was always chatting to God, often as I ran about or danced around in God's creation.

My brother and I would stand in the dark chocolate mud at the beach, wriggling our feet till they disappeared in its softness. We'd climb the stairs of tree branches, perching up above passers by, enjoying our hidden, secret place, and the different perspective from it. I'd be allowed out with my grown up sister in the gathering darkness on snowy evenings, to slide over the glistening whiteness in our orange-crate sledge. I'd peer into the diamonds of water caught in lupin leaves after rain. I loved the bright crimson raspberries as the sun shone through them over my head in a private den. My Dad and I would sit on a stile and notice all the different tones of green we could see. From my bedroom I'd watch birds nest building and then feeding their chicks. I'd sit at the top of the stairs and let the coloured light from a stained glass window make coloured patterns on my knees. I used to dance around the garden singing to the plants, explaining that God had made them and loved them; I thought they had a right to know!

We children played for hours in the wilderness next to the church in our road. It was like a small wood, with a grassy patch in the centre, which we'd use for summer Brownie meetings. As Margaret and I were friends with the vicarage children this wilderness was also our private playground.

CHAPTER 3

GROWING IN FAITH

Both my parents loved books and music, and I think I also met God through them reading to me. We would climb on Mum's lap and she would read from Winnie the Pooh stories and poems, with all the different voices; it was always acted out. We just loved those story times, and would often all end up crying with laughter. Mum later told me that at St Bernard's she had been introduced to A.A.Milne's stories as religious books, Christopher Robin being like a God figure, and all the animals so affectionately loved.

Dad would make himself into an armchair with his legs as my armrests, and read or recite poetry to me from *Palgrave's Golden Treasury of Verse*. Long before I could read I was loving poetry by Shakespeare, Milton, Blake and Wordsworth. I suppose it was partly because I liked the music of the words and rhythm, partly because Dad understood them so well, reading them beautifully, and partly because of simply sharing lovely times with my Dad. Sometimes he'd say "O little Sue, I do love you!" And I'd reply,"O great big Dad, you've made me glad!" I'd caught the rhyme and rhythm bug very early on. When I read those poems now I'm struck by how powerfully faith shines through, often as an unquestioned given, and wonder if I was growing in faith by a kind of osmosis!

My favourite film was *Robin Hood* as I enjoyed the adventuring and Robin's principles! I also loved Charles Dickens, Geoffrey and Henry Treece, and some of the books read on Children's

Hour – *Tom's Midnight Garden*, *The Wonderful Adventures of Phra the Phoenician*, *Carbonel*, and *Jennings and Derbyshire*. And as I got deeply into ballet, from ten onwards, it was all the Sadler's Wells books. Eventually I was hooked on the Bronte sisters, Rudyard Kipling, and *Robinson Crusoe*.

Throughout my childhood my parents helped me by showing that, though they didn't always like what I did, their love for me clearly wasn't affected. I can remember furiously screaming and stamping my feet in one of many tantrums, while my mum calmly carried on knitting until I'd calmed down, at which point I'd get hugged and taken to a new activity so that before long I had forgotten my fury. A wise woman, my Mum! I also remember something unusual about my Dad. He was increasingly in a lot of pain from his legs and this made him increasingly short-tempered sometimes. What I remember, though, was that if this happened he'd make a point of coming and apologising to us children, not trying to excuse his behaviour. He had a lot of humility, I think.

Although Dad went to church on a weekday near the Guildhall in the City where he worked, and Mum went to a local midweek communion service, on Sundays we children walked up the road to the nearest Sunday School, while Dad worked on the allotment and Mum cooked the dinner. My sister had been sent home from Sunday School for chatting and laughing, though as she has always been a brilliant mimic I wouldn't be at all surprised if she'd been practising this gift, which wasn't always appreciated! I couldn't hear very well then, so I never knew what we were supposed to draw as we knelt on the scuffed floor in front of our green canvas and curved metal chairs. Instead I made rubbings of the canvas with the paper and wax crayons and have no memory of ever being asked what I'd drawn! My brother joined me at Sunday School when he was three. He sat there with his legs dangling and in the silence called out loudly, "LIBERTY BODICE!" Maybe this was the rudest word he knew. Or maybe he just liked the sound of it! We were both bundled off home and my parents didn't send us to Sunday School any more. This wasn't the kind of church they felt was helpful.

Instead we started to catch the 6A bus on Sundays along with the Catholic families, to St Alban's, the nearest Anglican church to us where God's loving kindness and forgiveness were imbibed through word and sacrament, through the senses, as well as the bible. Never having been anywhere like this before I was surprised and happy to find that the God worshipped here matched up with the loving God of Creation I already knew from the garden, the countryside and the sea. There was a very small Sunday School held in the vestry during the service, but I much preferred being in church. All I remember of the Sunday School was my sister, me, and our cousins doing our best to make fun of the teacher.

In church, people were calm and reverent, and in their reverence I felt that we were all in God's presence. Of course I didn't understand the words, but I loved the music and candlelight, the times of stillness and shared worship.

In fact it was during communion, as I watched the elderly – including my Nanna Morris – making their way slowly to the altar, as we were singing

> Let all mortal flesh keep silence,
> and with fear and trembling stand
> Ponder nothing earthly minded,
> for with blessings in his hand
> Christ our God to earth descendeth,
> our full homage to demand…

…it was then I realised that the God of kindness, love, nature and family could be worshipped in a church as well as outside. I'd never thought this was possible before. My previous experience of church had been a place of strictness, rules and a load of half heard muffled echoes that meant nothing to me, whereas outside I quite naturally experienced God's presence very strongly. I've always remembered this moment in church as being a milestone or cairn in my faith pilgrimage. Maybe you remember your own faith cairns?

There were times at school which nourished my faith as well. One song we sang in assembly I specially liked. It was this:

> Daises are my silver, buttercups my gold
> These are all the treasures I will have or hold...

Another favourite was this:

> Over the Earth is a mat of green,
> Over the green the dew.
> Over the dew are the arching trees
> Over the trees the blue.
> Over the blue, the floating clouds
> Over the clouds the sun,
> Over it all is the love of God,
> Blessing us, every one.

Of course I realise now that both these songs spoke to my sense of the natural world being magical, holy and alive.

All kinds of people we meet influence us in our faith journey too. When I was seven all my infant school friends moved up to the juniors, but because my birthday was in September I had to spend another whole year as an infant. My initial fury and disappointment disappeared when I met our teacher, Miss Isaacs, who was so kind and patient, and seemed genuinely fond of us. I loved the way she read us Worzel Gummidge stories, and taught us as if we were already grown up. I was chosen as Mary in the nativity play that year – probably because I was one of the oldest, I expect. Also I could sing in tune. But I remember being told by another teacher to smile with my mouth closed because I had lost so many teeth! Miss Isaacs would never have said this, I thought, and her loving, wise thoughtfulness taught me so much more than just the curriculum.

There were special friends as well. My friend Olive and I share the same birthday, which we used to celebrate together in our flat. I loved having a twin friend to share this special day with, and my Mum would make a shared birthday cake for us. Dad organised the games. When we were still in the Infants, Olive and I made up a whispered poem for the silence after the playtime bell was rung.

"Olive Carter, be my partner."

"What for?"

"Marching down the corridor!"

During playtime a whole crowd of us would play skipping, or handstands against the wall, or hanging upside down on the bars. My friend Pat was also a neighbour so we rigged up a cocoa tin and string telephone between our houses, pinging the string to get each other's attention. We also dug a tunnel under the fence, which wasn't seen as such a good idea! Pat and I dragged long grasses up to make a nest in a tree and we'd lie up there in our nest and read or chat. My friend Linda and I made a market stall and sold what we'd made for charity.

One year I wrote a nativity play script. Dad negotiated with Grandad for us to have rehearsals in the garage, Mum helped us with costumes, Margaret played carols on her recorder, and Dad and I made posters. I was so well supported. Finally we arranged all our chairs in rows in the living room and turned the bay window into a stage area. Mum served mince pies I think, and all the parents came. It was a real performance, and such fun to do.

At church there was a visiting missionary from the Gold Coast with a deep booming voice and wonderful stories of Africa. His name was Father Cyril Barclay and he became a family friend. David and I were taken to the circus at Battersea, and to tea and toast at his Old Harrovians club. He was a member of the

Barclay banking family I later discovered. At the time what impressed me more was that he was quite a good magician.

I'd always loved browsing Hamley's magic tricks section, so he had to watch all my efforts at conjuring, which he did as if he was really impressed. I had tried out my floating sugar cubes on our vicar, and he solemnly stirred them round and then ate them! (Well, he probably pretended to eat them.) But his calm, boring reaction had put me off. Father Barclay was suitably amazed by my disappearing penny, and matchbox pet finger.

I could imagine becoming an African missionary myself, and I started to read up about Africa in our heavy volumes of encyclopaedia. I remember David and me being put on the train at Victoria and being met by Father Barclay at Felpham where he and his family lived. It was close to the beach, where we jumped around in the breakers, and I was surprised to find that one of my favourite poets and artists, William Blake, had lived here too. We passed his house on our way to the beach.

I was first published in the *Church Times*, with a letter and poem about our church.

> In this St Alban's jubilee year
> Three thousand pounds we need I fear.
> If I should get five bob from you
> It would help a bit, so I hope I do.

I did!

My friend Janet and I celebrated being seven by getting the bus to the local high street and back. We sat upstairs in the front seat and felt very grown up. When Pat and I were leaving primary school we wanted to go for a day trip to France on the steamer from the end of Southend pier. Pat's Dad very kindly accompanied us, but kept his distance so we could feel we were really on our own! I remember kissing the ground when we reached Boulogne. Such an adventure.

CHAPTER 4

GROWING UP

Like my Mum I chose to go to St Bernard's Convent, rather than Westcliff High, where all my friends were going. I liked it being a home as well as a school, not only for the nuns, but also for boarders from the Congo, and from Lille in France. Mother Vincent would sell us ice cubes of lemon or orange squash in the summer. Mother Mildred had been headteacher when Mum was at school and she was still head when I was there. I remember her knitting white stockings while we ate our lunch, and early on I was summoned to her knitting desk after lunch. I'd been doing handstands as usual. I was told I couldn't do that any more because I was showing my knickers!

Some of the girls in my year had been to the prep school and others to the catholic primary, so I knew no one when I started. There was a bit of bullying. I can remember refusing to be tipped off a bench in the playground, however violently I was pushed. But it wasn't long before the friendships grew, helped by the way I could play my recorder by ear, so they'd ask me to play all the latest pop songs, and they'd sing along as I played and twiddled. The other thing I soon became known for was making up songs and poems, and drawing, so they'd come to me asking for a personal song, or a portrait, or a poem about their boyfriend. I'd always done this, like my Dad, so it came as a surprise that it wasn't something everyone could do. What I found was that it enabled me to make friends across different groups, and accents, which I enjoyed.

Penny and I were – and still are – very good friends. We both loved ballet, drama and dressing up. Her family lived in a house with an attic, where we often acted out stories dressed in whatever came to hand. They also had a piano which they never seemed to mind me playing. I'd only play by ear, but loved finding chords to accompany my one fingered tunes. Her mother and grandma were jolly and theatrical and her father an army officer.

Although I often cycled to school, I caught the bus if there was ballet after school, cookery, and P.E. all on one day. As young people we were still expected to give up our seats on the crowded bus to older people, even if maybe they weren't carrying anything. Often we'd be lurching down the bus with our arms full, feeling like laden Christmas trees. My chosen alternative was to walk, saving the bus fare to buy a Wagon Wheel at break time.

At church in my confirmation classes, and at school, we were taught to pray each morning, and I never managed this, so I used my walking time to catch up on the praying I'd forgotten. This probably meant that I spent far more time in prayer than I ever would have done if I'd said prayers as I was told. Isn't it interesting how our faith journey often progresses quite randomly, or even through our mistakes?

I prayed for each home as I walked past, much as I'd done with the flowers in the garden as a young child. I was happy to thank God for the natural world I loved – trees and grass, sky and clouds, rain, and the wild flowers managing to grow in junk-filled front gardens, or in window boxes. Puddles with reflections have always fascinated me, and I used to think of nature like a puddle reflecting God, many years before I eventually discovered Saint Clare, or Saint Bonaventure.

These mornings of a solitary half hour walking and praying formed a foundation which developed my sense of the spiritual, even though I'd only started it because I disliked falling about in the bus, loved Wagon Wheels, and never managed to remember to pray when I woke, as advised. I suppose for me, pilgrimage became an early pattern of prayer.

I'd also started to go with Dad to evensong, which he had to go to as he was now a church warden. We sat together in the back row, next to the warden's wand, and there was plenty of scripture to read, and several psalms sung. Dad obviously relished some verses as beautiful, others as funny – I could tell by the way he sang them, and I enjoyed working out when to change the note in the unmetrical Anglican chant. Some of the prayers I still use were absorbed by heart at this time, such as the the General Thanksgiving Prayer.

Our family stayed at St Alban's church, although as soon as we were able to cycle to St Margaret's at Leigh, my brother and I joined their thriving youth club, called AYPA (Anglican Young People's Association). Being a member involved attending evensong, and we ended the evening with compline back in church.

It felt good to be part of a larger group, and as I was at the lower age limit, there were plenty of older members who played guitar, or were about to set off to college or university. In discussions here I had to up my game as you needed to know what you were talking about, which I rarely did. We also went on hikes and pilgrimages, met up with crowds of other young people, and of course, formed relationships. Several lifelong marriages started with that AYPA, including some of my friends, and my brother and sister-in-law.

We still went to St Alban's on Sunday mornings, and enjoyed acting in the drama group as well as washing up, which suited us all well, as the kitchen became a flirting opportunity. I remember visiting Walsingham and being drawn into the mysticism there, and the earthy business of having water poured over our hands and into our mouths. It was probably at this stage that I wondered if I sensed a vocation to become a nun. Had it not been for the necessity of renouncing the Anglican Church and accepting papal infallibility I would probably have become a Catholic. Eventually, having fallen in love, I decided I had a vocation to be a vicar's wife! Becoming a priest didn't even cross my mind, as it simply wasn't on the menu. I still wanted to go to Africa, and got all the details for VSO.

This was the only time my Dad absolutely put his foot down and refused to let me go. I was hoping to go to the Congo, which was often in the news for its violence and murders. Eventually we came to an agreement. I'd put VSO on hold and take my gap year after college instead.

CHAPTER 5

ST JOHN'S VICARAGE, FULHAM

During each holiday, three times a year, we lived in Fulham. The reason for this was that Father Harry Greaves, the young curate at St Clements, had become a family friend ever since that time. To me he seemed like a Grandad. When his wife died, and he was a vicar in Fulham, one of his daughters and family lived with him in the vast, cold vicarage on Dawes Road, and each holiday they would stay with their friends and family, while we took over. The vicarage, though rickety and rundown, was enormous. I'll show you around.

Opening on to the street was a large entrance hall, like a miniature Kew Gardens, with glass roof and patterned, tiled floor. This led to a large hallway with a huge shiny gong we could bash to summon everyone to meals. Off this was a kitchen where Mum reckoned she marched several miles to make a pot of tea, and a dining room containing a huge polished wooden table round which we all fitted with ease, a mirrored, polished wooden sideboard and several other pieces of Victorian furniture. Also on the ground floor was a big study, with desk, bookshelves and armchairs, a huge living room with marble fireplace and piano, and, behind a door, was a staircase leading from the hallway down to the basement. David and I spent plenty of time down here, playing table tennis, or hiding in the food hatch which could be hoisted, creaking, to the dining room. We could then tumble out to surprise everyone, though no doubt they had heard our journey long before we emerged.

Leading up from the hallway was a rickety oak staircase, good for sliding down the banisters as it covered three floors. Upstairs were two bathrooms, one green and one blue, a freezing television room, many bedrooms, and on the very top floor, up a narrow flight of stairs, was the attic, where a lady lived who I think was a deaconess. She was always happy to see us, and let us play with her many string puppets. We learned to work them eventually. From her attic you could climb out on to the roof and see the view over London.

All the downstairs rooms had heavy wooden shutters, painted cream, which had to be clanged shut each night and opened each morning. The garden had a high brick wall, which we'd climb so we could sit high above the people walking below. Raspberries and blackcurrants grew in the garden where the black cat – Charles, Duke of Cornflakes – caught mice. David and I would buy a ticket for one stop on the underground and see how far we could travel on the tube before getting out. Or one of us would take the tube, the other go by bus and we'd agree to meet somewhere like Harrods, Hyde Park, or the museums. We also enjoyed going up to the roof garden on the Derry&Toms store.

Our shopping in Fulham was done in North End Road, where all the stall holders called out greetings to Father Greaves, striding along in his cassock, smoking a pipe, and they would often give him presents of fresh fish or meat wrapped in newspaper. I remember Mum having to scour the cookery books to learn how to cook a whole salmon, something she'd never had to do before. There was often wine with our Sunday lunch – all gifts from parishioners, I think. Father Greaves told us some of the pastoral stories. One I remember was about him visiting a man who lived in a tenement, and insisted he wanted nothing more to do with God. This was taken as an invitation rather than a rebuff, and many times Father Greaves toiled up the stairs until eventually he was invited in, and helped that man, who became a faithful member of the congregation. I imagine all the stall holders, who clearly loved him, would have similar stories to tell.

Sainsbury's was tiled and spotless, and you queued at each different section for dairy products, meat or biscuits. At home we usually bought broken biscuits, but here it was whole ones which weren't home baked.

The congregation on Sunday was very diverse. Huw Weldon, at that time head of the BBC, stood and swayed through the hymns in the row just in front of where we all sat. Wealthy people invited us to their grand homes in Holland Park, and David and I used to be ushers at the African and Caribbean weddings, when the church was vibrant with colourful clothes and rich spontaneous harmonies. The congregation never needed the hymn books we offered as they knew all the words by heart.

At Christmas and Easter we'd help decorate the church till it smelt like a garden, and my Dad, who was a server, would light all the candles till the place glowed. When we were alone in the church I used to try singing from the balcony, and he helped me learn to project my voice. We made friends with the young servers, and watched the boat race on the Thames from Bishops Park, as the smell of beer wafted over from the south bank brewery.

Living at the vicarage was colourful, lively and eventful. You never knew what would happen next. The kettle was always on the hob, there were always people at the vicarage after church, having a sherry, until Father Greaves pulled out his watch and asked "what time's your lunch?" They always took the hint.

Although he could never read music he played his piano beautifully, and composed several Mass settings and hymns, none of which were ever written down. As he played, his cigarette ash would fall down on to his cassock, and he'd sing along with his playing, the cigarette somehow still in his mouth! He also walked around the garden praying, especially after his regular visits to the Royal Marsden cancer hospital, or the hospital where people were treated in an iron lung. As I overheard the many ways people had been helped by prayer, and had even recovered after receiving the sacrament (he would touch their lips with the Host and consume it himself) I was privileged to watch God's reality played out in the real world.

One year after midnight mass we got back to find someone copiously urinating against our front door. One day I discovered that the murderer, Dr Crippin, had lived in the next street. People would often come to the door with their stories of need, and Mum gave them tea and cheese sandwiches, while Father Greaves listened and gave them the fare to the nearest centre.

One day I answered the door to a man who explained that he'd had his tools stolen. While I wondered how to help, Father Greaves came striding down, laughing, and hugged the man at the door. It turned out the man was one of his friends, another vicar, just pretending to tell the kind of story they had both been told so often.

Whenever I was back at school in Southend I used to look out of the high window of our form room towards London and imagine it all going on without me.

CHAPTER 6

ST BERNARD'S CONVENT

While I was at St Bernard's, Vatican 2 took place. The nuns were very excited, and the school hosted the first ecumenical Christian Unity meeting. I remember it well. On the stage was a table, behind which sat a Catholic priest, an Anglican vicar, a Baptist minister, a Methodist minister and I think a Congregational minister. All men, of course. One by one they stood up stiffly and said who they were and what they believed. Then they sat down. It wasn't much but at the time it was heady and courageous for them even to share the same platform. I could see this was the very beginning of a groundbreaking journey. I think we even prayed the Lord's Prayer together – probably each denomination in our own familiar words – but at least we were praying together. It was a start. Mum and I were jubilant.

We had a school chapel, and all of us attended a regular school Mass at St Helen's church, next door. At that time it was all in Latin, which became familiar and normal after a while. I also remember sitting at the back of the classroom in French lessons with my friend, making a DIY ouija board to discover who our next boyfriends were going to be. It didn't occur to me that this in any way ran counter to my Christian faith. The nuns hitched up their habits to play tennis, and when I was doing French A level our teacher, Mother Mary Stephen, had to get dispensation to teach us books that were on the Pope's list. I think this was because they were existentialist, rather than immoral!

In RE lessons Mother Maureen encouraged us to ask questions and we'd have lots of discussions, which I enjoyed. I never remember the nuns telling us what to believe. The nearest we got to that was if our discussion hadn't resolved, and our teacher might say, "well, my dears, it's a holy mystery!" What our nuns seemed to want was for us to think for ourselves, which gave us plenty of freedom and allowed us to avoid becoming clones.

Social gospel was important and encouraged though, and many of us campaigned for justice, raised money for local and international charities, and helped out at local care homes. As I learnt more in history, geography and in the books I read, I became increasingly horrified by the injustices of the past and present, and ashamed of being part of a country where slavery had been so casual and destructive. In my own family history I was uncomfortable to find I was possibly descended from a diamond mine owner in South Africa. I was thankful and proud that our family was considered poor because we lived in a flat, had no car, television or fridge, and didn't go on holiday.

Helen Mirren was a couple of years above me, but even her early performances in our House plays had us all in tears. She was very kind to me when our Art teacher was off sick for a long time while I was in my GCE year. She was doing Art at A level, I think, and looked after us and taught us unofficially. I'm sure she wouldn't remember me, but I'm very grateful to her!

I was asked to talk to a class of Catholic girls about the reformation, from my Anglican point of view. I can't imagine I knew much about it really, but I enjoyed getting a discussion going. Already I had decided I wanted to teach. This had been partly due to some excellent teaching I'd experienced, as well as some terrible teaching, and partly because as soon as I learnt anything new I found myself working out how I could best explain it to others. Long before, I'd successfully explained long division to my brother in terms of trains, which he loved, so presumably it had already registered from an early age that the language of teaching needs to match the thinking of the learner!

By the time my schooling finished, I think I felt confident in my faith, optimistic about the future, ready for anything and convinced I'd be able to change the world.

CHAPTER 7

STUDENT YEARS

As I had made up my mind to teach I wanted to go to a teacher training college, rather than university. No one in my family had further education, and I wasn't encouraged or helped, but I was lovingly supported. In many ways this was an advantage, as it taught me to explore for myself, and make my own decisions. I chose Chichester, where what is now University College linked to Sussex was then Bishop Otter College, already linked to Sussex University. This was a church college, which I wanted, and in a beautiful part of the country, far enough away from home for me to be independent, but not too far to go back home to visit my family and boyfriend. I was eligible for a full grant, a luxury compared with today's situation. It was one of the first places to offer an honours teaching degree with equal weight given to education and your subject. My BEd from Sussex was in English and Education. I couldn't decide whether to go for Art or English, but chose English because I knew I would always paint, but maybe wouldn't get the opportunity or the inclination to read so widely. As subsidiary subjects I took Music and Drama.

I loved my time at college. At first it seemed as if we were on holiday after the full-on time doing A levels. Living residentially there was plenty of time to explore the surrounding country, and talk with friends late into the night. I also continued writing poetry, publishing in a local poetry magazine, and meeting Robert Gittings who was very encouraging and a great mentor. We'd have poetry readings with guitar or sitar music in the basement students' union, washed down with Guinness.

Here are two of those short poems:

SUN

Tangled among the branches hangs a sun
Which though diluted, pale and somewhat cold
After its evening blooded heat, is one
And the same, for each new sun is old.

TREES

Trees in the rain are dull green and bulky
Fastened in graded rows of gauze against the sky
Which closer acquaintance
Finds to be speckled with leaves.

And this is part of a longer one…

CANAL

Glide quietly under the water
Where reeds upended thickly curve;
Narrow wires, wind-laced and crazy-regular
Stutter the slurred smooth wetness
Of the sky.

In this wet softness
Let me drift and lie
With minnows passing
And passing minutes expressed
In the speckling dance
Of the darting gnat.

Here let the grey sun sift
In deep grass resting,
Heavy with secret jaws.
Let the grey canal
Regard the lines,
Observe the signs
Of morning sinking
Between the berries.
And evening rising
To meet the rising gull.

Reeds, weave thinly the greased canal,
Needle straight-backed through the sky
And by the waving image
Prove the wind's reality.
Sift the green among the silver
Clasping the damp and clamorous sun;
Sift the mist in grey disturbance,
Heavily breathing, life begun.

I won't bore you with any more!

I was still a hopeless timekeeper and remember my tutor giving me an alarm clock in desperation at my constant lateness! The newly developed foundation year gave us the opportunity to experience learning completely new skills, so we could both learn and analyse the way we learnt. We would see a process through from start to finish, and I still have a belt which started as a fleece, and was washed dyed, carded, spun, woven and finally stitched. I carved a wooden bowl, made sculptures from salt, soap and stone, made a wooden dulcimer from scratch, and played with coloured cuisenaire rods to experience Maths in a new way. Sussex was innovative and exciting, and we were willing guinea pigs. I have continued to use many of the methods, and certainly the excitement of learning, ever since.

Here are a couple of poems I wrote at the time.

LITTLE CHILD

Little child wanders, barefoot, barefoot,
Face now serious, face now joyful
Looking at the world that we have made them,
Looking at the characters we have produced.
How can we, without splitting your silence
Enter your world, little child?
Shouting may startle
And anger may open your eyes very wide.
But only the quiet reminder of childhood,
Only the part that is always the same
Can enter your world and enjoy it all with you.
Little child must meet little child.

And this was a lullaby I wrote for my brother's first baby

Rock-a-bye baby, the sky is a pool.
The leaves, slightly blurred are translucent and cool.
The sounds of the garden hang clear in the sun
And your life, little baby, has hardly begun.

When the wind blows the seasons will pass.
Autumn will scatter the leaves on the grass.
Before you is much that you don't understand
So rock-a-bye baby, hold tight to my hand.

Being a student in the sixties also meant being part of a culture shift. So much in our background made us politically aware, passionate about peace and freedom, wary of the dangers from mass obedience, and with a collective sense of breaking with

43

tradition. Making love not war was not just a slogan for us, it felt more like we were pioneers of a new and better age. And we were waking up to the beauty and fragility of our planet home.

While I was at college Auntie Edith died. To us this was both a surprise and a relief, as it meant we wouldn't be evicted. We had never formed a relationship with her so I don't remember any sadness. And Grandad started behaving differently towards us after her death. Dad persuaded him to start going out again. Mum cooked and cleaned for him. Then he began to visit The Plough and often the police would bring him home, very drunk and disorderly. Mum would clean him up and somehow cope. After a year or so Grandad died of the alcohol. I didn't go home for his funeral.

Father Greaves also died. He'd been mostly living with us after retirement, and he was visiting his home at Burton upon Trent when he died. He'd been such an inspiring mentor, friend and Grandad to me, and I cried a lot when he died. I was given permission to go home from college so I could be at his funeral and the cemetery, which I still visit sometimes. He was no saint. I knew him with all his faults and failings, together with all the generosity and kindness that came from his close relationship with God. I have so much to thank him for, in my journey of faith.

The degree was a four year course which meant I had four wonderful years of living in Sussex, including joining the archaeology team working on a cemetery outside Chichester, and at the Roman villa at Fishbourne. Our climbing club would tackle the Swanage cliffs and Welsh mountains. I learnt to sail in a leaky Enterprise dinghy in strong winds. My boyfriend Bruce thought I was a natural at balancing the boat but actually I was desperately trying to avoid falling in the water! We also did bell ringing, horse riding and plenty of walking on the South Downs, both by day and by moonlight. I helped at the local mental hospital, and sang in the chapel choir, which was led by the cathedral organist and choirmaster. For some lectures we'd go to Sussex University at Brighton, and in my final year my friend Anne and I rented a pretty mews cottage in St Martins Square. On Sundays I worshipped at the cathedral as well as the college chapel, and ran the Student Christian Movement until I became an atheist.

CHAPTER 8

ATHEISM

Writing this now, I want to think carefully about why I became such an evangelical atheist. It was not that I drifted away from church gradually. I didn't.

A number of different factors gathered to this point in my faith journey. My current boyfriend Bruce had been insistently and often violently arguing against my faith for a long time. (Yes, I probably should have read the danger signs, but I didn't.)

In Education we were studying Philosophy and Psychology, and I found I could just as easily argue against the reality of God as for it. The book *Honest to God* had been published, which seemed to me to discount the God I knew and loved. Our 60's culture was taking seriously many of the values I had thought of as Christian, yet Christianity for many was associated with what I had rejected as a child.

So, starting with the latest theology which seemed to be unaware of, or to deride, the personal relationship with God that I had, I too began to think of God as not so much person as concept, and that I could argue against quite easily. And I did like arguing. I always wanted to dig out the truth, even if it was uncomfortable. The last thing I wanted was to be taken for a ride. After all, I prided myself on being sensibly sceptical and not easily fooled.

We were staying with another couple during the Easter holiday in Southwold in Suffolk. With my head and heart in confusion over all these ideas and arguments I went to church on Easter morning. The flatness of the service, and the unfriendly congregation (as I perceived it) clinched it for me that day. As darkness gathered, Bruce and I were on the beach, and the arguing began yet again. I had no appetite for it, and felt finally beaten. There and then I spoke aloud my decision.

There was no such thing as God.

It wasn't true that God was the creator.

Humans had invented God, not the other way round.

It was a terrible moment and one which still hurts to remember. I can almost hear the angels weeping. Suddenly I realised we were alone in the universe, and the emptiness – the absence of God - was appalling. But I had to be honest, and honesty compelled me to reject everything I had known, experienced and loved all my life.

Immediately I stopped going to chapel and the cathedral. I resigned from the Student Christian Movement. I changed some of my friends. The college chaplain invited me to his office, where he listened, but probably wisely made no attempt to change my mind, and we remained friends. Christian Union members assured me they were praying for me, and I laughed at such absurdity. I'd sometimes go to their meetings and pompously ask questions I knew they couldn't answer, just to show how clever I was and how stupid they were.

My love of the natural world became something to fight for, as I could see the environmental dangers looming. I took up the hobby of the ouija board and enjoyed being in touch with the dead. At least, that's what it felt like! I did my best to persuade believers to grow up and recognise the truth. The truth as I now saw it. I am sad to say that I sometimes succeeded. As I said, I was a very evangelical atheist.

CHAPTER 9

MARRIAGE NUMBER 1,
AND A MOUNTAIN

Bruce and I had been planning to live together when we finished at college, and had no intention of marrying in a church, making vows in the presence of a non-existent entity. So, at the end of our final year, just as the moon landing revealed our vulnerable and amazing planet in its beauty, and instead of going to Africa as a missionary, my friend Anna and I hitch-hiked around Norway while Bruce worked in an ice cream van, and my Dad suffered a stroke. He was taken to St Bartholomew's hospital where at that time there was no rehabilitation programme or physio. We married at the local register office and came back to Stondon Lodge garden, where Mum had prepared food and drink for the very few guests. No one from Bruce's family came. I wore the shortest dress I could find, and on our way to camp in North Yorkshire we visited Dad in hospital. He still couldn't speak, but tears filled his eyes. I gave him my flowers.

We moved to Buxton, in the Peak District, renting a cold flat above a fish shop on the high street. Day and night Scammell lorries full of limestone changed gear outside our window, as we were on a hill. Opposite, the market sold carpets, meat, clothes and cheese. I was teaching at the girls' grammar school – Cavendish. In the snow, sheep would wander down into the netball courts. We kept snow shovels ready, and the local teenagers would stand at the bottom of the hill and take bets on how far the cars would manage to drive up before they got stuck.

There was a very lean September before we got paid, and for a few months before emergency tax was sorted out. We camped in the flat as we had no furniture, and just enough food. It was an exciting day when we bought an old gas stove at an auction for two pounds, and found a chair discarded on the street, which I covered in some cheap fabric from the market. We'd sit in sleeping bags and cut people shapes from that crispy toilet paper, which danced in the fishy draughts coming up between the floorboards.

We had chosen to move here because of the opportunities for climbing, caving, mountain walking and white water canoeing, so there was plenty to do at weekends, now that I no longer went to church. We made our own neoprene wetsuits and I particularly loved the canoeing in the Derwent river at Matlock. I had learnt to canoe on this river in January. We would work our way upstream, ferry gliding from slack water to slack water, then have the exhilarating charge downstream, reading the water so as to avoid the rocks.

This was a poem I wrote at the time:

> Shout mountains!
> Laugh and chatter and dance for once
> Instead of pretending
> you never endeavoured to move.
> Look at the water and learn it from him.
> Break out of your silence and sing!

We also went ice skating, loved the local auctions, and became regular members of the folk club. We ran a youth club on Monday evenings and I marked essays while I sat in the laundrette.

Bruce taught for a year at a primary school before deciding teaching wasn't for him. He applied to drive a limestone lorry, pretending he had experience, and turning a loaded lorry on its side on his first day. I remember his melted jacket! The company accepted it and gave him some tuition in heavy goods driving. It was a very stormy year and a half we spent together, violent and sometimes terrifying, before Bruce left to become a cowboy in Calgary, Canada. He left me a record of the song he felt was appropriate… "If I can't forget you, I may not come back at all…" I was never sure it was 'can't' or 'can'.

I was devastated when he suddenly left. In spite of the violence and abuse, I loved him. I loved the untamed wildness of him, the way he always chose the most dangerous things to do, and the craziest way to do them. Everything was an adventure, and if it wasn't, then with Bruce it soon became one.

I remember a van crash in the ice and snow, when my head smashed through the windscreen and my knee through the dashboard. When I became conscious again I thought I was dead. Then I thought Bruce was dead as he still wasn't moving. But we survived. I remember climbing frozen streams up waterfalls, right to their spring at the top of the moors. Bruce's parents ran Keld youth hostel in Yorkshire, and we had explored there often, never using footpaths, but clinging to crumbling valley sides, and skinny swimming in rock-pools, often at night. He'd play a mouth organ or his Jew's-harp by the roadside as we waited for another lorry to take us on the next stage of a hitchhiking journey. And suddenly he was gone, leaving a huge sense of loss and rejection.

I reacted with a mental breakdown, which meant I missed half a term of teaching, became suicidal and couldn't do anything or decide anything. It felt as if I'd fallen into a precipice and had no idea how to climb out. I was afraid I had gone mad, but the psychiatrist explained that in view of all that had happened (which I haven't bored you with) it would show insanity if I had not reacted. What I was experiencing was a sane reaction. I suppose it was a bit like PTSD.

And what about my faith journey in all this?

Well, I'm sure many people have made the transition from faith in God to humanism which has helped them become kinder, more loving, compassionate and accepting. For me it was a different story. Possibly because my Christian faith had never been strict, authoritarian or exclusive, I had not been in rebellion against a false notion of God. Instead, and probably worse, I had first-hand experience of the power of God's love, and had made the deliberate decision to turn my back on that, rejecting the One I knew loved me and all creation.

So I became increasingly hard and unkind. Like my toddler self in tantrum mode, I think perhaps I was being as obnoxious to the non-existent God as I could! With Bruce leaving, there was a crash. Living in an abusive relationship, and without faith, I had reached the end of my own resources, and had nothing left to fight with. Certainly I have experienced a lot more since then, but never again felt like that.

Climbing out of the mental precipice was a long haul. It was helped by my lovely Mum's phone calls, visits and belief in me. Getting back to work was scary, but healing. The choir helped. Walking in the hills helped. Gradually I was recovering. I remember laughing for the first time in months and how strange it felt. I have kept paintings and drawings from that time which are very precise and decidedly unsettling.

It was the following summer that I joined a cross-Europe camping trail to Morocco, and on this trip made the decision I had probably needed to make months earlier. If I was to move on I would have to accept that Bruce and I were no longer a possibility. Yes, of course that hurt, but I knew it had to be done if I was to recover fully. The fug of marijuana in our four by four, the overview of Europe and the contrast with Fez, Marrakesh and the Atlas Mountains were probably the best rehab I could have had! I nursed my need for acceptance and affirmation by having numerous partners and challenging myself to discover my limits in wild and probably dangerous ways.

By the autumn I felt more alive again, loved the teaching, walked in the hills and mountains with the local rambling club at weekends, and felt stronger for having survived the Bruce experience. A new teacher at Cavendish needed accommodation so now she shared the flat with me, which was excellent. I was asked to devise a new Environmental Studies course for some sixth formers from the girls and the boys schools which was great fun. The Duke of Edinburgh Award Scheme was just starting up, so I was involved with that. I did my Mountain Leadership training, and RYA so I could also teach sixth formers sailing on the Errswood reservoir. I volunteered at the local youth centre, where they wanted me to play with different arts and crafts, so the young people got curious and soon joined in. That suited me fine. I enjoyed their company as well as experimenting with pewter, clay, printing and glass painting.

That winter I took a school group to Austria for skiing, and in the summer we booked a Mediterranean school cruise for about 25 girls. I think there had been a fire on the ship we were booked on, so we went ahead designing our own teaching on an ordinary cruise ship with a Greek crew. We three staff had to take turns to patrol the corridors at night as the girls and crew were keen for adventure. I remember walking at the back of our group through Beirut, with a male teacher in front. Clearly the locals assumed he was selling us all, and there were plenty of offers of transistor radios and camels.

As part of this cruise we visited Israel, and swam in Lake Galilee. It felt strange to be here in the place Jesus had lived and worked, seeing the hills where he went to pray, yet being separate from these events since I didn't believe. I had no problem with accepting that a person called Jesus had lived here – there's plenty of proof for that anyway – I simply saw him as completely human, and found it sad that so many people, including me, had been persuaded to believe in a lie.

A science teacher at the school was a Christian and of course I was back arguing with him. The music teacher never argued, but just cheerfully lived her faith, and against my better judgement, she did impress me! I was told I had to teach lower school RE which I tried to get out of, being a very outspoken atheist. But it had to be done. So there I was, teaching mainly Old Testament as if I was teaching English. And I did love the English teaching, and made the most of all the theatres around to organise visits to plays and films in Sheffield, Manchester, Liverpool and Stoke. I loved it when students would catch the depth and joy of literature, the drama, the poetry and the prose.

One evening I felt an unusual, strong urge to go into a church, but waited till dusk so I wouldn't be seen. The church was still open. I sat inside. It felt quite weird to be in a church, and I didn't really know why I was there. But I liked the peace. I had been getting into Buddhism and trying to meditate, but annoyingly kept finding Jesus getting in the way. So I'd given it up. After this rather secret visit to church I started to go to spiritualist meetings sometimes. I'm not sure why. Partly because I wanted to debunk it, I think. One day the speaker had a message coming through for the lady in the red raincoat. That was me. He said I had a problem of wearing my heart on my sleeve which had caused me pain. He said the message was from my Grandad (he used his name, and phrases Grandad often used). And he said I would soon be changing my job and would become well known.

Well, I took most of all that with a pinch of salt, and assumed he was making it up, or picking up signals from my appearance. I was quite annoyed at him mentioning a change of job as I had not the slightest intention of leaving teaching! But I didn't like the way people were warned of their future, which I felt was unhelpful and possibly detrimental to them, so I stopped going to the meetings. Instead I would go to the Quakers sometimes as I found sitting in the silence helpful and not challenging.

The next summer I decided to drive my white minivan and tent to Scotland and walk back home to Buxton down the Pennine Way. The science teacher and his family were going to camp at Kirk Yetholm and I rather hoped to meet them there. As it happened they had already left, but I set off anyway, looping my way round so as to combine walking and driving, and camping either in the open or in campsites along the way. I walked the whole of the Pennine Way like this and there was plenty to see, I had lots of adventures and there was also time to think. I suspect I was still recovering, really.

One day on this long walk I was climbing Ingleborough hill in Yorkshire. At the top I stood and looked out at the view, not thinking of anything in particular when something happened that changed my life for ever. Suddenly I was aware of someone standing just behind my left shoulder. I felt their physical presence and I knew who it was.

Now I know this sounds crazy, but I knew it was Jesus, quietly standing there with me on the mountain. I felt his hand on my shoulder. I wasn't frightened, I wasn't angry, I just felt his peace healing me. I remember saying, "okay, you win… it is true then… I think I'd better get to know you better!"

When eventually I was on my own again I felt very different. I felt happy and relieved, lighthearted and kind of freed up. It was utterly extraordinary. I ran and jumped down to Ingleton, ate lunch at a pub, and felt so full of energy and excitement that I climbed all the way up again, feeling completely free!

In this poem, which I wrote later, I was remembering something of my bewildered wonder on that Yorkshire hill:

HERE

Here on the fell top is the great Earth's edge.
Its grit and limestone wrinkled into hills
And valleys spreading skywards from your feet.
Its movement from the reddened, dipping sun
A ponderous roundabout.
Mere gravity to strap you in, or else
Ride off and out through wide, unblinking space
Past trembling stars and silent distances
Which measure growing oaks as opening flowers.

Petals, bright and fading
Seas and snowflakes
Dust and thistledown
Drift past these rocks, and rain,
While tangled sheep's wool ruffles in the wind.

Stand watchful on this planet as it rolls
Through lifetimes, terrors, hopes and anguishes
Contracted in its long protracted birth:
This place is where the Christ himself would pray;

Creator on Earth's rim of aching hills,
With field lilies round his sandalled feet.

The rest of my Pennine walk was wonderful, with a lightness in my step, people I enjoyed meeting, and unusually for me, keeping this bubbling secret to myself. When I eventually reached home and got into bed, I started to pray. "Hello God, it's Susan," I started. I sobbed as I apologised. I wanted to pray more, but didn't have a clue what to say. I went to sleep eventually. Next morning I woke up with a new, clear thought in my mind. I'm afraid I hadn't thought of this before, but now it occurred to me that my Mum was at home looking after my Dad, since his stroke, and if I wanted to, I could go and help.

But I hadn't wanted to. I'd much preferred to be totally independent. As this new thought settled into my mind I realised it had happened directly after my fumbled prayer. That shocked me. And then I thought back to the presence of Jesus on Ingleborough. I began to realise that acting in response to my prayer was the way Jesus could and did communicate. Maybe, then, he'd been there all the time, whether I'd decided to reject him or not! Maybe he had even been there on the beach that night when I had chosen to deny God's existence. It was quite a heady thought. Almost too much to cope with at the moment.

So I put it to the back of my mind, and got on with living. But I did act on that waking idea. I arranged to give in my notice, explaining that I was needed at home, and I would leave at the end of the school year. I applied for a job near Southend at a comprehensive school in Basildon. In May I went down for the interview and was successful. I was to join the Humanities team, teaching English to GCE at O and A level, but also teaching those who couldn't read or write. At home my Dad understood that I would be coming back home, and I could tell it made him happy.

A week later my Dad had another stroke, followed by a heart attack, and died. I went back home and managed to see him before he died. It was almost as if he'd been hanging on to life until he knew I'd be back. I wondered if I had been nudged to visit that church, and Jesus had met me on Ingleborough so that I could be back home before Dad died. I am so very thankful to my Dad for so much. I still miss him! At his funeral I felt that part of me had died with him.

CHAPTER 10

ESSEX

So I left lovely Derbyshire and came back to flat Essex, living in Stondon Lodge with my Mum. Although I hadn't been able to help her as she looked after Dad, at least I was there as she grieved. In any case my sister Margaret had been wonderful, forging a better relationship with Dad as his nurse than I think they ever had before. Mum and I went that summer on a wine tasting coach holiday through France, which gave us plenty of time to sit and talk, as we drove through beautiful country, and stopped frequently for vineyards, cellars and tastings. It was good for both of us. At home I had a bedroom and sitting room of my own, which suited us well. We had our own space even though we often chose to spend time together, especially in the garden.

At school the staff room was full of characters, crazy jokes, and a wonderful range of different people. The teaching was challenging for us all, which made for a therapeutic staffroom humour! My head of Humanities was a History teacher who had recently returned from Kenya, where he had been teaching since finishing at Cambridge. He played rugby, got brilliant exam results with his students, and was dynamic, well liked and altogether larger than life. And yes, it wasn't long before I moved in with him. At that time teachers were still expected to marry if they lived together, so soon afterwards we faked a marriage, I changed my name by deed poll, and my long-suffering Mum gave us tea and gingerbread. Amazing how expectations have shifted since!

As you probably noticed, it hadn't taken long for me to discard Jesus' personal invitation. Here I was once again leaving my Mum rather than choosing to stay and be there for her. Self-centred behaviour takes such a long time to change. I did now drive my Mum to church each Sunday, but I couldn't see it mattered if I was late picking her up.

Gradually I came to stay and sit with her, rather than making another journey, so it was a year or so later before I started going to church for myself as well as my Mum. It really disturbed me to be in God's presence. I found tears pouring down my face as I started to receive communion, and eventually plucked up the courage to talk to the vicar about it. What he suggested was that I could renew my baptismal vows, and he would write to the bishop requesting that I could receive communion again now that I was a Christian. I was also given a cross to hold in my pocket, and a tattered copy of *Jesus Revisited* by Malcolm Muggeridge, which helped.

But this big sea-change took a lot of courage for me to do. I found it very scary. Was I really ready to commit myself to being a Christian?

Well, in the end I decided I was as ready as I would ever be, and I did it.

I felt literally as if I had been born again. It's hard to explain, but the sense of being accepted, loved and cherished by the universe Maker who I had rejected for years, but had met in Jesus on Ingleborough, was like becoming a new creation myself. It was humbling, happy, and totally extraordinary.

This is a hymn I wrote at the time:

LOVE AND FORGIVENESS

Love unchanging, all containing,
Great sustaining love of God.
For on soil which love created,
God, through love, incarnate trod.

Caring, tending, all expending,
Love unending here we see
As Jesus, man and maker,
Gives his life to set us free.

Cost incurring deepest sorrow
Offering constant yet complete
Such unqualified compassion
Drives us weeping to his feet.

Undeserving, vain and foolish
Love exposes us to be
Yet with arms outstretched in welcome
Jesus greets us tenderly.

O the sweetness of forgiveness!
O the bleakness filled with joy!
Cascading from the heart of God
Which nothing can destroy.

CHAPTER 11

MARRIAGE NUMBER 2

Not long after this we really did get married. I think the truth was that I now wanted us to be married. The vicar suggested that I should apply for an annulment of my previous marriage, so we could be married in church. At that time the Church of England did not marry divorced people. But I still wanted total honesty, and couldn't bring myself to declare my first marriage as non-existent, difficult as it had been. That simply wasn't true. Instead we arranged to get married at a United Reform church, where remarriages were allowed.

I want to affirm that my husband was and is a good man, highly principled, and honest. He is rightly admired, respected and valued as a fine teacher and lecturer, friend, tutor, and family member. I know this and I share it. You also need to remember that I am writing about my own faith journey, and my experience in this marriage is all part of this, which is why I am referring to it.

I had been warned by colleagues that he was a heavy drinker and suffered from depression, but I shrugged the warnings off. Having survived Bruce I felt able to cope with anything. Also, I was certain that when he experienced being totally loved, everything was bound to change. (Yes, I know now that doesn't happen, but this is what I thought at the time.) Now, we would better understand the mood swings and obsessive behaviour which he couldn't help. Alcohol had started as self medicating, but of course that made matters not better, but worse.

There were strict rules about our wedding which I readily adhered to. Only very few people were allowed to come. Apart from a couple of his friends, one of his sisters and her husband were invited. I was to wear an ordinary dress which I wore to work, and there would be no pictures. It was just before Christmas, and snowy, so I was ringing round for an available taxi. After the ceremony my husband went to the pub with his brother in law, and Mum helped me arrange the food at home. I remember crying into the gammon.

So why on earth had I landed myself once again in a problematic relationship? Both these men have so many very fine qualities. But both struggled with quite profound difficulties, and I am pretty sure I must have made it worse for them. Bruce had left me after only eighteen months, but I saw in this second marriage a fresh start, and wanted our vows in God's presence to be a life commitment. Rooted in God's love, our love would surely make that a lifelong pleasure.

And certainly we shared many happy times, and our love deepened. I don't need to go into detail but it wasn't easy for either of us. I have no doubt that I could have managed differently and far better, but we still loved each other and both of us did our very best. As well as the difficulties there were also the good times, which were very good. We stayed together for nearly twenty years.

What I really want to look at in this story is my faith journey, and of course our marriage had consequences for that, so now you can think of it as a backdrop to all that happened next. It certainly had the effect of giving urgency and depth in my life pilgrimage which might not have happened otherwise. I learnt when to speak and when to shut up and be quiet. I learnt to recognise the hidden pain that is so often disguised by prickly and violent behaviour. I learnt to cry out to God and how to find God's answers in scripture or in our personal parables of the everyday. I learnt so much about how God can be trusted.

63

This is a poem I wrote at the time, which shows what it felt like at this point in my life pilgrimage.

I AM THE WAY

Surprisingly it was not hard to find,
Existence once acknowledged possible.
It stood out from the landscape, raised and clear.
A sea wall snaking through the distance,
Sunswept and exposed. No maps or signposts
Necessary here. The way is simple:
Find the limits of your land and walk along.
That deep eternal water by your side
Is there to guide you and direct your path.

Heady with the wine of this wild place
Which sang through consciousness
To depths I felt, but could not understand,
I ran towards it, stumbling in my haste
And scrambling through the grass and brambles till
I stood up in the wind and watched all those
Who made their measured ways along.

It was a path made beautiful with flowers
Springing up where gentle feet had trod
And patient feet, and feet
With perseverance stoutly shod.
My own were scratched and torn.

I started eagerly, exhilarated,
Loving the spray washed air
The reeds wind laced
The curlew's arching call,
Wondering at the joy the burdened wore.
The steadfast concentration in their eyes
As if they walked

Through wilderness or fire.

Then gradually I found that for me too
The Way was turning dark and inhospitable,
The going rough
Strange shadows all around.
The wolves' howl menacingly near.
I stopped in fear.

'No, Lord,' I said, 'There must be some mistake…
Give blizzards, storms, harsh cold or caustic heat
But not these terrors I cannot control.'

I felt his hand upon my shoulders placed.
I saw him shake his head and smile.
He offered me his hand and on we went,
I concentrating now, committed more
Than I had ever been, dependent
For survival on his grace.

The darkness closed in shapes and thorns around.
I heard the wolves approaching
Saw their fangs.
Though he was there, they had not disappeared.
They hunted still. The kill was in their breath.
But now I had begun to understand.
The Way was Love.
With Love they might be tamed.

Certainly I was now able to write with working knowledge of
what it meant to cling on to God for dear life. As I said earlier,
this time was far harder to cope with than my first short
marriage, and yet now I was constantly buoyed up by God's
kindness, and protection. I learnt to be aware of the hidden
pain beneath the surface cursing and rages. I learnt the value

and urgency of a constant undercurrent of prayer, and the mindfulness which pays attention and respect to the moment. I learnt what forgiveness means, and how Jesus' burden is weirdly light even when things are darkest. I learnt how to cry out to God and find God's clear answers in scripture, or like Jeremiah and Amos, in the personal parables of the everyday.

This was a hymn I wrote at the time

> Lord, when I turn my back on you, the fears and darkness grow.
> I need you, O I need you Lord, to show me where to go.
>
> With you beside me Lord I find the evils that I face
> Become instead a joyfulness, a fountain of your grace.
>
> So shape me to your purpose Lord, and tell me what to do
> And when I start to turn away, then turn me back to you.
>
> And when the world is over Lord, or over just for me
> There is nowhere but your heaven Lord where I would rather be.

So much of what I wrote during that time grew out of my gradually emerging knowledge of how God's love is real, makes the impossible possible, heals and holds, protects and comforts, even gives joy and thankfulness in the darkest places. I was writing from personal experience and I know that has helped many people, who probably had no idea of the background. God works so powerfully through the difficult times we struggle with. We can sometimes think we need to work FOR God, but of course the real miraculous truth is that God works FOR us, so we can then speak out as witnesses who have seen and experienced that love first-hand!

CHAPTER 12

PARENTING, PRAYER AND HEALING

Mothering two incredibly wonderful children was such a delight. The way a baby's expressions change all the time, and you can watch them and love them for hours on end. The way their personality develops, almost as if they are uncurling from the foetal position. The delight as they start to talk, make jokes, ask endless questions and speak such profound wisdom, with uncanny innocence. Getting to know these small people is an absolute joy and such a privilege. They have always taught me so much, often made me laugh, and helped me in so many ways. They still do, as do all the grandchildren!

When I had stopped teaching to have our first daughter, there was far less available time than I had naively imagined, but I started to read the bible a lot. This felt urgently important and although I didn't know why, I did it anyway. I found it gripping, actually, and there seemed to be so much more value in reading it now than when I was younger. I also joined a group at our local church, arguing as usual, and challenging them constantly. I was a real pain! The fact is, I still hung on to a deeply embedded scepticism, and remember saying that if it was really true, surely Christianity would look more like I had been reading in Acts? Surely there would still be healings, and changed lives, and speaking in tongues? They looked at each other and then at me. Well, they said, it was all happening, and I was welcome to come with them and see for myself. That's how I ended up in the charismatic movement, which I hadn't heard of before.

All around me was real, deep worship. Expectant faith. And as the worship and teaching continued, I heard the lovely sound of people singing in tongues. Now this was amazing, because I had been praying like this on my own for several months, swept up into worship with love and thankfulness as I read the words of scripture. Now I discovered I wasn't alone, or a freak. (Well, perhaps we all were!) I joined in, released in a way I hadn't been since hippy days, but now the focus was not on me but on God. It was wonderful. And all this in someone's ordinary sitting room. The silences were deep and holy. I felt I had come home.

Obviously all our faith journeys and routes are different, and speaking or singing in tongues isn't a badge to wear. So many have found their faith expressed differently. But for me, this is what happened!

For years the girls and I worshipped at our church on Sunday mornings and at somewhere charismatic in the evenings. We went to Spring Harvest each year. We'd book first, then pray for people to fill the booking. It always worked out. One Saturday evening before Pentecost I was worshipping with some Catholic charismatics at someone's home. There was no whipping up of emotions, just some calm teaching from Soul Survivor's Bishop David, and a diverse group of people focused, expectant and attentive to God. We stood in silence and prayed for God's Holy Spirit to fill us.

It was as if a wave of God's power swept through the room. I found myself on the ground, as were others. Without any forcing, I found myself not crying, but 'being cried'. I couldn't stop. I didn't feel sad, it was more like being healed without surgery. A couple of people knelt and prayed with me, content to let the Holy Spirit do what needed to be done. As suddenly as the crying had started, it stopped, and all the insults I was used to experiencing daily at home had vanished, especially the heartache of rejection. This was God's extraordinary kindness and love in action, healing where I most needed to be healed, and equipping me to go on. Every Pentecost I remember this outpouring of God's generous love.

As the girls grew up, and after we were living on our own, we went to Dorset, where the Soul Survivor camp was happening. At the time I often needed to wear a neck brace. This was a result of a previous whiplash injury and the hospital had told me the damage was considerable, and was unlikely to get better. As I could no longer move around easily, let alone lead the physical worship at holiday club, this wasn't good news. But it didn't occur to me to pray about it. I think I felt this injury had resulted from my own stupid fault, so God wouldn't be interested!

That evening, in the packed hangar which was the main worship venue, we were sitting near the back. Bishop David was explaining that healing was God's gift, so anyone open to God could be a channel. There shouldn't be rich and famous people standing out as having the gift of healing. We just had to all get used to the idea of really being open to God, rather than getting in God's way.

So as to demonstrate this he asked for a few people to join him and for all of us to pray that first section of the Lord's Prayer: 'Father, let your kingdom come. Let YOUR will be done'. And to mean what we were saying. Then he said there was someone – maybe more than one person – who had a problem with their first and second vertebrae. He asked them to make their way to the front. Well of course, that was my problem. But I couldn't bring myself to walk all the way to the front. So I stayed where I was. I was relieved when someone else went forward.

Even so, now as we all prayed the same, simple prayer, and the people laid hands on the person, my own neck began to feel warm, and I realised that God was healing me as well. It was a complete healing, and I have never needed a neck brace since. It also meant I could energetically lead the children's worship when we got home. I love the words of the general thanksgiving prayer… "that we show forth thy praise not only with our lips but in our lives…" After such healing, how could I do anything else!

In subsequent years the girls and I would drive to New Wine, where they would join their friends and camp, while I went on to the Franciscan Friary at Hilfield, where I'd camp on my own and join the community, working in the vegetable garden or the kitchen, and using the library and surrounding countryside. I had become a Third Order Franciscan, and I have valued this ever since.

CHAPTER 13

WRITING

I had stopped writing poetry and painting early on in our marriage, as creativity was an unmentionable concept in our house, and I was happy to accept that. But after Pentecost, when the girls were still young, I started writing again, submitting some poetry to the parish magazine. Our vicar thought I should see if these poems could be published by Kevin Mayhew, who worked nearby at that time. I had been composing poems and a carol, and one day dropped them through his letterbox. I heard nothing, and needed the words of the carol, as of course I hadn't thought to keep my own copy. So I phoned him and asked for my work back, please. Kevin rambled on about how many offerings they received and how there was a difference between what worked locally and what would work in a wider market, but he'd phone me back when they found my work. After about half an hour he did phone back, and he was laughing. Weird, I thought. I just wanted my carol back. But Kevin expressed his apologies, said they really liked what I'd written, and did I have any more? And could I come and see him?

So that's how I started publishing with Kevin Mayhew, and becoming good friends with this crazy, dynamic, impossible and lovable man and his lovely wife and children. Our friendship has spanned forty years. Now I began to understand why I had been nudged to become steeped in scripture. Kevin wanted me to write books to help Catholics who were starting to explore the bible readings for Mass, and needed some ideas. But, I explained, I had no theological training, and had never written resources for worship. No, he agreed, but I was a communicator, and that's what was needed.

I was still quite a new Christian, and my Mum agreed to type out what I wrote if that would help. She was the only person who knew what life was really like at home, and said that, reading between the lines, she could see where I was coming from.

I chatted my way on paper through the Mass readings, all three years of them, with many different versions of the bible and commentaries spread out around me in a big circle, and several people I would phone when I still couldn't make sense of what I was reading. The books I was writing were called *Focus the Word*. They sold well, and they had taught me such a lot. Eventually my Anglican and Methodist friends were asking if I would do a similar resource for them as they were having to adapt these Catholic books. When I suggested this to Kevin he didn't think Anglicans would buy books. But because the Catholic ones were selling well, he let me have my way. So I wrote *Springboard to Worship*, and it sold so well that Kevin changed his mind about Anglicans!

After *Springboard to Worship*, other resources followed. Most of the books are really praying and teaching on paper, and although I have mainly taught in secondary schools, once I had children of my own I felt less terrified of teaching younger children. My favourite has been teaching all the age groups together, and I was often asked to take training days where this happened.

The invitations came through the books I had published, and I travelled widely at this time, sometimes arriving just in time to launch straight into the day. I think I was able to do this work because the royalties were income, so were acceptable. I would often bring the girls with me to training days, so the value of working with different ages together was obvious. I learnt so much from all the people I was there to teach. I saw their faith, listened to their questions and comments, and was impressed so often by the way they embraced what was, at the time, quite a new challenge for many churches.

Kevin and I would discuss the needs of the church, and he had a remarkable gift for pinpointing what would be useful. We didn't always agree of course, but that all helped further discussion! I also learnt a great deal from the children and young people at church. I remember one Christmas seeing one of the three year olds scooping up straw in the Nativity crib, and went over to stop him throwing it. Thankfully I only asked him what he was doing. He went on scooping straw and patting it down to cover the baby. "I thought Jesus looked cold," he said.

O my goodness, how much we learn from young children! I remember once getting really frustrated trying to fix the toddler seat on the pram, and my toddler stroking my leg and comforting me, saying "never mind, mummy, the fresh air will do you good!" And I remember once at church finding the holy water stoup was empty, and my youngest stretching up, dipping in her hand and crossing herself as she said in a matter-of-fact kind of way, "but it's full of holy air!" Too often we adults think we need to teach the young children when so often it's the other way round. No wonder Jesus appreciated the little ones, and even used them as a teaching example.

I would try out my latest ideas on the children and watch their response. If it worked for them I'd use it. If it didn't, I'd discard it. Sometimes when I'd been writing all day, the ideas would have become more and more crazy, so by the time the girls got home from school they'd suggest it was time for me to do some long division!

And how did this stage of full activity impact on my faith journey?

For many of us, there are some stages of life when we are constantly busy. For me this meant I got up just before 5am, took my pot of tea to the office/library/spare room and prayed. Then I wrote or did essential teaching preparation till 7am. I was wife and mum till nearly 8:30am, teacher till 4:30pm, mum and wife till 7:30 or 8pm, teacher till 9:30pm and catch-up time till bed. I would have two days when I wrote instead of teaching, but I know that for plenty of us, constant demands are just part of life, and in many ways we love it. Although we naturally get tired, it's a good feeling to be in demand, with plenty to do, with responsibilities and challenges all day long.

This season of life is all part of our faith journey, I think. Work is Prayer. We get plenty of practice in learning how to listen, when and how to act, being honest about our successes and failures, inspired by the examples of others we meet through each day, privileged to share in other people's struggles and achievements, and perhaps above all, we can practise living in the moment, which so often helps stress management and enables us to learn that undercurrent of prayer. That's why I always found it so important to begin the day with making contact with God, sometimes in words, sometimes silence. The most urgent need was to cultivate being in God's company, so this could continue through whatever activity happened to fill the rest of the day's moments. I found it increased my thankfulness, stopped me from holding on to everything, enabled me to kind of look inquiringly in God's direction as I made the constant decisions, in many of which I knew I needed God's guidance.

Much of my writing work involved reading the bible imaginatively, listening to the subtext and reflecting on what it might mean for those hearing it today. Particularly as I was writing resources for preaching and teaching people of all ages and faith stages, it was very necessary to stop frequently and remember that God already knew and loved these people. The books I was working on wouldn't be published and in use for probably another year, and so I simply had to ask God to give me the words which would help whoever was going to be using these resources. The intercessions – prayers – had to 'be prayer' in their making, and I often completely lost track of time. But ever since, people from all over the world have told me about how something in those prayers spoke directly to them and helped them pray. So what an amazing privilege that God is willing to use us whoever we are, with all our faults and weaknesses, and all we need to do is be attentive and listen!

I wouldn't like you to think I always listened, though. Far from it! A learning process is a bumpy journey involving plenty of getting lost, falling over and insisting the wrong way is right. And I've done plenty of that. But even those are a training ground, where we gradually understand more and more of how God's loving kindness and mercy is not out to smash us down or reject us, but to rescue us again and again. Steadfast love. That's what God shows us, and he teaches us faith by always having unshakeable faith in us!

Loyal friendships were invaluable, and one particular friend stands out, though all were wonderfully kind and understanding. Christine and I had met long before, and I remember her being baptised when she was about twelve. Later on, she and I were both pregnant at the same time, and finally her daughter was born a short time before mine. Those two have been friends ever since, as have Christine and I.

CHAPTER 14

CALIFORNIA

In 1986 our family moved to California for a year. It was a teaching exchange arranged by the Fulbright programme so we were exchanging homes, cars and jobs. This meant that we were immediately part of a network and community, which was excellent as we wasted no time on settling in. It was also the happiest, calmest year of our marriage. The girls went to the local school, along with many Mexicans, and my husband taught at the high school. I continued writing and also joined the community college to study music. Eventually the girls were placed in the GATE programme at a different school on the other side of town. They also joined the Methodist children's choir and the Suzuki violin group.

We went mainly to St Dunstan's Episcopal church, where Sunday School for everyone took place before the main service, and I also enrolled on an ecumenical bible training course at which about a hundred working women met weekly, were taught by a woman theologian, and were allocated discussion groups. If you missed a session you missed getting the handout so weren't allowed to join in the discussion. Three misses and you were out, as there was such a waiting list. We were living in the great valley, between San Francisco and Yosemite, where most people went to some kind of church, and bible study was considered essential. At our class they took me aside and suggested I become a group leader, on condition that I wasn't divorced, and didn't speak in tongues. I had to confess to both so the offer was withdrawn. Nor were these fine, well-educated women allowed to teach men, which accounted for the all female membership. (There was another large group for the men, with male teachers.) But it was valuable teaching, and I enjoyed those Monday evenings, reading the prophets.

I also got invited to speak at various different denominations where my books were used, so I remember breakfast sessions with the Catholics after Mass, hands-on sessions with the Methodists and Lutherans, and biblical studies with the United Reform Church and our own Episcopalians. Before coming to California I had been wanting to discern God's will about women becoming clergy, as I really didn't want to get in the way of God about such an important matter. So I had decided to make my body completely still for half an hour in church each week, to aid stillness of mind and heart, fearful of how easy it would be to end up not listening at all. I continued this in California, and was, I confess, quite shocked one day on sensing God putting into my mind 'what if I asked you?' I shot back, 'well you couldn't, it's against your rules!' O dear me, I hadn't really been opening up to God at all, had I? So, as many times and situations before, I just ignored it and carried on enjoying what I was doing, and assuming that nudge had been a mistake, or my imagination.

As our year in California drew to an end, a letter was sent to our priest which he shared with us. It was from Barbara Butler, Bishop Tom Butler's wife, who had set up a group called Christians Aware. St Dunstan's millennium was coming up and Christians Aware had written to churches dedicated to St Dunstan around the world, inviting them to take part in a pilgrimage from Glastonbury to Canterbury the following May. As we would be back in England by then, the girls and I decided to take part, representing St Dunstan's Modesto. This pilgrimage turned out to be life changing – yet again!

Walking all day with a diverse group of people from different countries and cultures gives you plenty of time to talk and listen, share and discuss as you walk. With the changing countryside as your backdrop, the flow of ideas and stories runs free. Relationships that would usually take years to develop are forged here in days. And spending two weeks living simply and in close contact with the rest of nature, gave us fresh insight into our 'normal' lives, with assumptions questioned, as well as the ordinary celebrated with thankfulness. Often we would find the local church community coming out to meet us towards the end of a day's walk, and we greeted each other like long lost friends, though we had never met before. There would be real conversations over welcome food, lovingly prepared, and we'd bed down on the floor of a church or church hall or local school, so wedged in that when one person turned over, we all did! And there might be one cold tap and one toilet, but there was always plenty of warm hospitality.

Here is a song I wrote on the way, which we sang sometimes as we walked:

Chorus

We're walking on a pilgrimage to heaven
And every step of the way you are here beside us.
Walking on a pilgrimage to heaven,
With the Lord our God as our guide.

Sometimes rough and stony
The path is hard and our progress is slow
Then bright meadow flowers
And sunshine as we go…

Sometimes feet are weary
And muscles ache at the end of the day,
Then good food and lodging
To cheer us on our way…

Not only was this a very happy time, but it was also a time when my faith was re-earthed. As you already know, I set out on my journey of faith as a young child, with an instinctive love of the Maker and creation, and during this pilgrimage it was as if I had met up once again with that sense of being surrounded by my human and non-human sisters and brothers, aware of being an integral, living, breathing part of God's whole creation. We have spent far too long mistakenly assuming that humans are somehow separate from nature, and once we realise the truth, it shifts our perspective and widens and deepens our faith in the Creator God.

We walked into the empty Canterbury Cathedral muddy, boot-scuffed, and singing. I remember how the sound was caught up into the high arched forest of stone as we, so short in comparison, made our way up to the choir stalls where we were to sit. We had walked our way across England, across stories, with shared worship, eating, sleeping, laughter and questions. We had retraced the life journey of Dunstan, made a thousand years before. This cathedral linked us through space and time back to the land where Jesus had lived, back to all those faithful story keepers down the ages, ordinary and footsore, grand and famous, wise and foolish, right and wrong. It was an honour to be part of the story.

CHAPTER 15

CHRISTIANS AWARE, FRANCISCANS, AND WOMEN'S MINISTRY

Barbara Butler invited me to be part of the Christians Aware annual conference, and, typical of Christians Aware's willingness to face the challenging issues of the day, I later found the conference that year was exploring the current issue of whether ordained ministry should be gender or person based. To be honest, I was rather horrified as I had been trying to keep out of this particular issue and I think I felt I couldn't manage any battles I didn't need to take on. But I was already booked on the conference, and trusted Barbara and Tom, so the girls and I set off for the CA conference in January.

How Barbara manages to get such excellent speakers to such a grassroots organisation I have no idea! I think maybe speakers are attracted by the multicultural, open minded, knowledgeable members. Over breakfast I remember chatting with Rowan Williams, who had just led a mind blowing bible study. And another morning I chatted with an amazing Mother's Union member from Lesotho, who explained that because of the steep roads and hills she travelled on horseback, lugging a generator to show health videos in rural clinics. Many people there at the conference who now lived in the UK had lived as missionaries in various countries, and you never knew who you might be sitting next to. I have been involved with Christians Aware ever since, and always that January conference, and the summer school, visits abroad and pilgrimages have kept my faith journey momentum going.

But that first conference made me look again at the arguments for and against the inclusion of women in ordained ministry. What decided me was scripture. In Genesis, the story of beginnings, creation began with light, but didn't end there. Instead there was a gradual unfolding, a development from the first day, and perhaps that pattern linked up with Jesus' promise that the Holy Spirit would lead us into all truth, and the passage from Ecclesiastes that there is a time for one thing and a time for something else. In fact the whole narrative of scripture is nomadic, tracing journeys.

Then in the gospels, there are clearly women among the followers of Jesus, and although the twelve (male) apostles mirror the twelve tribes of Israel, it was women who first met the risen Christ. Mary Magdalene is often known as the apostle to the apostles. Jesus' mother Mary had cradled the Christ so that, in a very real sense, she had a priestly ministry.

I had written this poem about her many years before when I was a new mother myself:

TO MARY

You who have washed the swaddling clothes
And hung them up to dry,
Ask of your son that patient love
Which perseveres, so I
May pour down the drain with this water,
Dank and baby stale, all my
Instinctive rebellion
At the call to sacrifice rights and try
To make of this washing a beautiful gift
Of love for your Son on high.

She was there at the foot of the cross, and in the room at Pentecost. In the early church, as recorded in the Acts of the Apostles, both men and women are involved in ministry.

But what clinched it for me was the burning issue of the time about Jews and Gentiles, and the insistence by some Jewish Christians on the practice of circumcision for non Jews who had become followers of the Way. This was a very important concern, and there were strong arguments on both sides.

What I value is the way it was solved. Paul gave evidence that the Holy Spirit of God was visibly at work in non Jews as well as in Jews. How then could we deny them recognition that God has clearly given? Their decision was made on this evidence, and gentiles were allowed to be accepted.

In 1990 I had tentatively made enquiries about the Franciscans. I have to admit here that I had kept their contact details for many years, but never been willing to use them. I think I was wary of the idea of Obedience. But anyway, I finally got round to it, discovered the Third Order, and went to see Pam, a shining Tertiary if ever there was one. I became a Novice, and was allocated a Novice Guardian who helped me through my time of exploration. Katherine Sladden was wonderful. She had taught in Poona, India for years, and was so good at noticing what wasn't said as well as what was. Calm and inscrutable, she was actually full of fun, and we grew into good friends. She even paid for me to join a pilgrimage to Assisi, which was a very lovely experience, and before I was professed, she engineered for me to take part in the York convocation.

This was held at the York University campus, and I remember feeling like a young kitten, curled up on heaven's lap that first evening, as the whole gathering of Franciscans settled quickly into silent adoration, because they were all so used to practising this at home. I also remember Bishop Desmond Tutu dancing arm in arm with Bishop John Dennis, as we all wound our way circling and singing to the top of a small hill, where we shared the Peace! Being a Franciscan Tertiary has been a central part of my own faith journey, right from when I danced around the flowers as a young child, singing to them about God's love.

One day, my friend Christine and I bought a static caravan in Suffolk, where we spent some very happy and necessary breaks. She was going through the ordination process and was one of the first women to be priested. St Edmunds Cathedral was jam packed, with marquees at the side for overspill. It was history in the making, very humbling, exciting and full of joy which had to be muted in its expression, out of love for those who had voted against this possibility. I hope the same muting of joy would have been expected if the vote had gone the other way.

Although we often couldn't travel abroad ourselves, we often hosted guests through Christians Aware and Host. Guests from India, Africa, Japan, Iraq, China and Europe came and stayed with the girls and me once we were on our own, and we were all greatly blessed by these friendships. We were also privileged to explain Christmas and Easter to those who had no knowledge of Christianity. I think this helped us focus on why we were really celebrating.

CHAPTER 16

SOUTH AFRICA AND A FRESH CALLING

When my uncle Eddie died, he left each of his nephews and nieces £2000. Finally the girls and I could visit South Africa, with a small Christians Aware group, so we would be staying with local families, and getting to know the people, as visitors and guests rather than tourists. We were all near Johannesburg. The girls stayed in Kwa Tema, and I was placed with Brian and Jane Luff in Nigel. Brian was actually the first 'Rainbow' priest, ministering in black, coloured and white communities, and Jane was nursing across the spectrum, too. What an inspirational couple they were, who taught me so much. I am very thankful for their example, their lived faith, and their extraordinary acceptance of me at that time. Their friendship is still a joy.

It was a significant time to visit South Africa. I have a copy of the voting paper which led to Nelson Mandela becoming president, and although wounds were still raw, there was a sense of hope and promise in a place where only a few years earlier there had been apartheid, persecution and fear. There were still townships, such as the one where the girls were staying, in which daily persecution had been normal, as we could see from the bullet holes, and there were still huge divides socially and economically. But Mandela's calm and generous wisdom was paving the way to a better future.

I remember receiving a standing ovation from the packed church of uniformed Mothers' Union when I visited the girls. The welcome and appreciation given to me was simply because

I was the girls' mother. They, of course, had become well known and loved in the whole community, just by being themselves!

I remember wondering what actually was wealth and what was poverty, as I shadowed Brian in pastoral visits to people radiating joy in their shacks, and others tense and fearful in their gated white communes. One day, after worshipping at Ulra Park, then a coloured community, a group of all ages climbed into a combi and we bumped our way through the township to bring Communion to those who were housebound. It reminded me of allotments in the UK, with homes like the sheds and patches of vegetables growing. We stopped at one home, and squashed inside, singing. The lady was very old and she was smiling and nodding as we sang. I could see daylight through the corrugated iron walls. It was clean and swept and full of God's presence. This was what being church was, and I had travelled thousands of miles to discover it here, in a corrugated iron house.

Later in this visit I was invited to join the confirmation candidates on their Cursillo weekend in Johannesburg. I was to be one of the supporting adults – the mommas and papas - and I had no idea what to expect. This was one of the first rainbow Cursillo confirmation weekends, and you need to bear in mind that all these young people had grown up in the apartheid system. Trauma was only just below the surface and healing was a major priority.

I can't tell you what happened to us all because Cursillo is always kept secret, so that when it happens we are constantly being surprised and challenged. I say 'we' because my role involved being part of one of the groups, so I experienced it all at first-hand, with no preparation. All I can say is that the overwhelming sense of love, trust and acceptance helped us all to face our ghosts and have them melted away. There were plenty of tears and laughter, times of forgiveness and fresh understanding, as well as forged friendships, as these courageous young people emerged stronger and resilient. In some ways these weekends reflected Desmond Tutu's brave and necessary Truth and Reconciliation programme.

Part of the time on this weekend was spent in teaching, and I was asked to prepare acetates for the overhead projector. As I drew the many hands praying over the head of an ordinand, I quite suddenly realised I had drawn myself. This was 1996, nearly forty years since I had wanted to be a missionary in Africa, thirty years since I had sensed a calling to be a nun and then a vicar's wife, and ten years since that quiet nudge in California, and I knew that this was no longer the time to argue my case with God, as I had been doing for years. Now I knew the time had come for me to say yes. And finally, I did.

It had taken all those years, the journey to this beautiful country and that beautiful corrugated iron home, and now this rainbow gathering of young, traumatised Christians, to reach this point in my pilgrimage. How tenderly God loves us and understands us. How patiently he waits for us. How he perseveres with us, surfing with us whatever crazy waves we choose to ride. And how he orchestrates timings and situations. I am still amazed every day by the sheer 'God-ness' of God!

My last few days in South Africa were even spent in a convent, where an enormous arrangement of flowers under the altar had been delivered to the nuns by their dear friend Desmond Tutu! Here in Africa, I had finally understood what it meant to be church. Immediately on our return I was booked to lead some all age groups at Caister, where the Chelmsford diocesan conference was held. The girls and I were given luxurious accommodation in a posh caravan, and the director of ordinands was at the car park when we arrived. I told him, and he beamed, telling me to get in touch. So my own journey to ordination began.

CHAPTER 17

TOWARDS ORDINATION TRAINING

It was another two years before I started training, and once again, God's timing was perfect, in spite of my protests! When the girls were both away at university I had put in place a couple of things to stop me feeling too lonely, as I knew I'd miss them so much. I joined a Scottish dancing class. It was hilariously hard to learn the dances, and I was always getting it wrong. But it was fun and we laughed a lot. The other thing I did was enrol on the Christian Studies course, mainly because I figured sitting in a group discussing things would be far nicer than sitting on my own with the cat. (Mind you, Molly cat was pretty good company as she talked a lot, and brought me many kind offerings!) As it turned out, the Christian Studies course was very useful, as a prequel to the theology degree. And it was indeed a pleasure to be part of a group each week, studying and discussing with mugs of tea and growing friendships.

In the area of writing I was in the process of working through the Common Worship lectionary. The Alternative Service Book had been expected to continue in the Church of England until Common Worship would be rolled out in 2000. We thought we had plenty of time. But then it was decided Common Worship would start earlier, in Advent 1997 with Year C, so that Year A would be in place by 2000. No spare time for us after all, then.

Kevin and the team took me to Lavenham for a wonderful lunch to talk about a revised schedule, and the tension was so strong that I couldn't eat much! The problem was that if we were to be ready with accompanying resources in time, the scripts would need to be submitted by June. It was already November and as I was writing the books, it was up to me.

Could I possibly complete four large books in seven months? It seemed an impossible task but I felt their concern. If we missed this deadline we would be missing a God-opportunity that couldn't be repeated. I imagine other publishers were having similar nail biting discussions. At the time I was also teaching, of course, so time was very tight. But it felt right to do it, so I agreed. Their relief was plain to see. As I drove home I explained to God that yes, I'd agreed (yet again) to an impossible task but knew that with God nothing was impossible! This was going to be God's work and could only be done if I allowed God to think through my mind, and guide me. Faith training in action.

Those *Living Stones* books did get done, as did the following two years of the lectionary. My friend Christine and I were on our way to Orkney as I dropped the final section of the final book off at a post office. By this time I was more of a zombie than ever, utterly drained, but also very relieved.

Orkney weather was closing in and I was due to begin ordination training in London the day we got back to England. After quite a journey, three different breakfasts, and the real possibility of not arriving until that first weekend had finished, I arrived only half an hour late, and the principal, David Sceats, met me at the college door. It was probably just as well that I had no idea of what we would be doing that weekend. When I walked into the lecture and discovered the whole of that first weekend was to be about Myers Briggs I nearly turned round to go back to Orkney. I had spent years successfully avoiding Myers Briggs!

Wrong again. That weekend set the stage for a truly valuable three years leading to a degree in Contextual Theology, and I was amazed to discover how useful Myers Briggs was for prayer, church council meetings, pastoral wisdom and generally acceptance that we are all different and so all need each other. I think probably I had been put off by not really understanding what this tool was. Gradually I came to understand more useful ways of communicating with others, accepting behaviour in myself which I had always assumed was simply wrong when actually it was just different. All are valid. Yes, even you! And all are part of God's love.

I was training at what was then known as NTMTC, the North Thames Ministerial Training Course. Each Tuesday we gathered for the whole evening, each month for a residential weekend and every year for a residential week. Nearly all of us were in full time work as well, and since we all came from different backgrounds and churches, we became used to translating what we said so it made sense to those from different traditions.

Our course took place at a very beautiful part of London, using Oak Hill College and their wooded grounds. As the M25 was somewhat unreliable for getting to college in time for worship and our evening meal, I preferred to leave earlier and continue writing, or doing student work, once I was there.

This place became my spiritual home, particularly welcome as I was no longer able to continue at my own church, since the vicar, a lovely, honest parish priest, did not feel able to have me there as an ordinand and also a woman. It was a painful leave taking, but had to be done, and that's why I so valued being settled here at college, where a whole range of traditions and theology were all recognised and respected. Often friendships blossomed across the differences. In many ways it reminded me of the comfortable acceptance of difference I had met at my school, St Bernard's, and at Bishop Otter College.

While I was at college my dear Mum died. I felt she had been training me to be a Deacon, as she had become increasingly frail, and needed more care. Margaret took on most of the care, and I'd often go round in the evenings. After feeding her and helping her drink and so on, I'd creep into church and find the altar laid and ready, with candles lit. Ever since, I've encouraged churches to avoid the usual last minute bustle, so that anyone in need of quiet welcome, as I was then, can come into God's presence and feel the expectant readiness.

I remember walking among the very old oak trees at college, just after Mum died, and receiving a really lovely sense of peace and love. I know that, like Dad, Mum always prayed for us all, and she wasn't about to stop now!

In our final year we went on placement. This was normally at a church with a different tradition from what we were used to, but as my writing had enabled me to worship with churches of many different traditions and cultures they asked me what I thought might be appropriate. I said either somewhere in Africa, or in a prison. They said in that case, it would be a prison!

CHAPTER 18

PRISON

Now I had assumed it would be a men's prison. I was currently teaching in a unit for those who were permanently excluded from secondary school, and I had always found adolescent boys much easier to teach than girls. So frankly I was rather horrified to find that my placement was at a women's prison, HMP Bullwood Hall. Warily I went in and was issued with keys and a leather pouch.

Then a surprising thing happened. I loved it!

It dawned on me that this might be why God had wanted me to move from the teaching and writing I loved. This place, with its noise and locked gates, metal stairways and small cells, seemed to be welcoming me. I carried on working in the prison chaplaincy for five years, a time which spanned my faith development as a theology student and ordinand, being ordained deacon, my ordination as a priest, and becoming a team vicar. So I'm going to clump together all the prison's five years before retracing my steps to those other important cairns in my life pilgrimage.

The chaplain, Janet, was due to leave soon, and she had been let down by a choir leader just before Christmas, so I was immediately installed as the totally inexperienced choir leader, with a Christmas concert looming. Every new inmate was visited by the chaplaincy within twenty four hours and that gave me a fast track to meet my parishioners. Prison life helped me on my own faith journey as I accompanied, listened, prayed, read the bible, and learnt from a remarkable group of people, both those sentenced and also the officers. We encountered more crises in a week than we'd meet in several months outside prison.

The prison was used for a television series called *The Real Bad Girls*, but quite honestly I hardly ever met anyone bad. Damaged, yes. Abused, often. Mentally ill, frequently. Often, lifers in for murder or arson would be grieving as well as dealing with guilt. And there were those who had been wrongly accused, for whom the experience must have been particularly hard. We never asked them anything about why they were in prison, but we often got told their stories. Some of those stories were harrowing and I would drive home in tears.

The choir was a release for all these women. We laughed a lot, always prayed together, and we sang our hearts out, with wonderful natural harmonies, like the singing I remembered from Fulham and South Africa. There were some terrific voices for solos, and each year I wrote a script for the Christmas concert which the rest of the prison came to watch. They didn't hold back on applause, but would also quieten down, listen and watch so attentively as their friends courageously acted out the Christmas story, and sang. The choir I belong to now reminds me of that vibrant prison choir. We also ran Alpha courses, adapted as necessary. Paul Cowley who has done such great work in prisons with Alpha, was a fellow student with me at NTMTC. I think it was partly through Paul that I ended up in prison chaplaincy as my placement.

Sometimes I'd jerk awake in the night, knowing I needed to pray. Then when I got to the prison I'd find out why I'd been woken in the night to pray. Our rounds always included those in the hospital wing and those in solitary confinement. Sometimes I'd wonder whether I was in a prison or a mental hospital, as so many minds had been damaged by drug use.

Even though the drug use may have stopped, the damage lasted.

Many people came to faith, or returned to faith while they were in prison, and we would baptise them in the swimming pool, or in the chapel if they preferred. As their sentence drew nearer to its end, some would dread being released as that would mean returning to the dangerous world that had brought them into prison. Some would know that the end of their sentence meant deportation.

The chaplaincy was multi-faith so it was imperative that I worked with many different faiths and traditions. There was so much we shared, and I learnt much from those of other faiths. Part of my role was to enable the prisoners' faith to be exercised and respected, which would often entail my presence at meetings in the chapel with their faith leaders who came in from outside. Some worship I could actively participate in, some not. I was often grateful for my own faith journey as I accompanied paganism, spiritualism, and humanism as well as the more mainstream faiths.

At that time the UK law was that application for asylum had to be submitted immediately on arrival. But this meant that those trafficked for the sex trade, who were kept as prisoners on arrival, had no right to apply for asylum once they managed to escape the sex trade. I contacted my bishop about this injustice and he raised the problem in the House of Lords so that thankfully the law was changed. That was a letter worth writing. In fact I often found I was a voice for the voiceless, and many were so good at helping once they understood the difficulties.

Bishop John Gladwin's wife Lydia, for instance, was such a help. She organised Mothers' Union members to transform visits for the women, by redesigning the space, and providing childcare when necessary. She was also a wonderful friendly ear who encouraged us in chaplaincy. Other support and loving care came from diverse Catholic Women's groups, who invited me to speak and asked for what was needed. Soon after, I received parcels of embroidery kits and knitting wool. It was such an immediate and practical response, I actually wept when what the women in prison had longed for, so quickly arrived!

Once I was priested I set up a midweek Communion service on Wednesday evenings. Sunday chapel services were always packed, mainly because this was the only opportunity for the women to get out of their rooms and socialise! (Close vigilance was vital, of course.) Lovely as this was, and a wonderful opportunity to spread the good news of God's love, I felt there was also a need for those simply wanting to worship. They had to apply for the Wednesday evening service and if I accepted the applications, officers would have the extra task of unlocking them and escorting them to and from chapel, so it was important to check the possibility of this. Consequently it took quite a while before it was up and running, and throughout this negotiating we were all praying for it to be allowed and feasible.

It was such a joy when we could begin! Candles were not allowed in prison apart from in the chapel, so I made the space beautiful with candlelight, flowers and quiet music as the little group of about twelve were escorted in. I had arranged the chairs in a semi circle and had been praying in this holy space from when I knew they would be starting their journey to the chapel. As they came in, there was often an intake of breath, sometimes tears. One by one they sensed my praying and we joined in silent adoration together.

This Communion service was like a taste of the heavenly for us all. It was spacious, holy, full of God's accepting love and kindness. Different people would read from the bible, intercessions were open for shared prayer, and we sang. When I was due to visit Bethlehem and Jerusalem again during the intifada it was this group who begged me to pray for them when I was there, and they promised to be praying for me.

As it happened, we were almost the only visitors there in Jerusalem at that time, and visited the church of the Holy Sepulchre very early one morning, before it was fully light. No one was there, queuing to go in, so I was able to enter, kneel, and pray for my sisters in prison. Never before had I thought of the resurrection so powerfully as release! Remembering each of the women by name, it was as if we were all there together, in the released glory of Christ's resurrection, even as I knelt in this dark, candlelit cell, no larger than the cells of those I brought with me in prayer. On my return to work, safe in spite of the dangers, I shared this experience with them and was able to thank them for their faithful prayers.

One day we were all gathered in the gym and told that Bullwood Hall was to become a men's prison. It would be emptied of women over two weeks, have two weeks for changes to be made, and then be filled with men over the next two weeks. For many of the officers and inmates this came as an unwelcome shock, and the chaplaincy presence was used to listen to the fears, comfort and reassure. I hope we did that wisely and lovingly. I was due to be marrying one of the women and her fiancé, and the governor kindly enabled this to go ahead, leaving this woman as one of the last to be transferred. So her wedding took place in an almost empty prison.

Once the prison was empty I sensed God's commissioning again. I strongly felt that God wanted me to do an important job. So, I went round the entire prison, praying in every room on every wing. It was an extraordinary pilgrimage. Forces of pain and evil, sometimes quite violent, would meet me as I prayed in the emptiness. I never knew what I would find. All I know is that accumulated grief, terror and remembered abuse are powerful, and hang around, and these needed to be dissolved by God's healing love before the next group of prisoners arrived. In some ways, as I think back, this was the most important commission of my life, and unless I had done it in God's presence I couldn't have done it at all.

The prison was a lot quieter and calmer with men, rather than women. Sadly I wasn't there for long after this, as I had become a Team Vicar, and couldn't manage to do both alongside my writing and teaching. But for me the prison chaplaincy work informed my growing faith, challenged me hugely and gave me so very much. In all the crises we faced together, all the pain and anguish I encountered, all the openness, resilience and steadfast faith, I learnt more about God's wide and generous love than ever before. I also learnt more about myself, recognising uncomfortable truths I hadn't wanted to visit before, but now, through the courage I witnessed so often in these sentenced women, I dared to accept and even forgive.

God wants us to forgive others, of course, but sometimes the other we need most to forgive is ourselves. I emerged humbled and thankful, disturbed and empowered, knowing vulnerability, but also determined, in God's love and truth, to speak out for those who have no voice, and not be silenced, even if it makes us unpopular. Even if we are, as some of those prisoners were, falsely accused.

CHAPTER 19

BECOMING A DEACON

I hope you are holding on tight now, as we take a sharp turn, back into my journey through college and ordination, as this too was a rugged path through the mountains, with wonderful views, companions and distractions, all of which is part of all our life pilgrimages. In a way we are like time travellers and maybe, like Dr Who, we regenerate through our bequeathed genes, and travel across times and places, so that our life span should really be measured in millennia rather than decades!

On our residential weekends at college we were given use of the study bedrooms of full time students at Oak Hill, which was an Evangelical Training College. All the character of each room reflected the personality of the fellow student we never met, even though we shared the same room and held each other in prayer.

Our Tuesday evenings began with supper, at which the the Oak Hill students shared the dining with us, followed by our worship in their chapel. We took turns to plan and lead this time of worship, so it was sometimes very traditional and sometimes very experimental, depending on who was leading. After chapel we went off to our lectures and seminars, with a fellowship break in the middle. We ended the evening with Night Prayer, gathering in a large circle and praying together before the journey home. I often remember roads being closed by the time we left college, and diversions were in place, leading us down lanes and through towns and villages I didn't know until eventually we were spat out somewhere not that much further on from where we had left the main road. At the time I was listening to the Harry Potter cd's, or we'd car share so our conversations passed the time as we travelled, and deepened our friendships.

In our residential week we became temporarily full time students, with enough time to talk over what we were learning, and relating it to our full time work. We began to find questions arising from our day jobs which helped us ground our theological studies. As it had been largely the Philosophy and Psychology which I had studied before, in my teaching degree, that had paved the way for me to lose my faith, I did wonder if the same thing would happen now, as once again we studied Philosophy.

As we did so I could quite see why I had come to discard the concept of God, but this time it was different. Partly through my intervening faith journey, partly through the many mistakes I had made and consequently my working experience of God's love, untiring forgiveness and acceptance, and partly because I was beginning to learn that arguing is not always the best way of approaching difference, I now found the studying fascinating but in no way dismissing the God I had come to know. Also, all my writing had involved many intense years of studying scripture as well, so I was getting better equipped, possibly. God is so kind to us, and so very patient!

Our three main lecturers were David Sceats, Ann Coleman and Tim Hull, and whether by happy chance or careful planning, these three completely different people provided for us a very well balanced diet of training. I valued their different styles and characters which prepared us so well for real life ministry. I found myself also balancing their styles with my way of responding. Let me try and explain.

David provided us with reams of closely printed prose on purple paper, and his detailed, academic knowledge in lectures was matched – or balanced - by my notes which were entirely drawings! It was the only way I could hold on to his meticulous scholarship. Ann was a creative contemplative who engaged with us wisely and shrewdly, cheerful, and attentive to our moods and needs. With her I could relax and let the teaching soak in. And Tim… well, I used to feel we needed to fasten our seatbelts as he swept us on a rollercoaster of questions and possibilities, using two screens and plenty of different visuals on each. He is quite severely dyslexic and I would help him prepare these exciting theological adventure rides by recording his dynamic ideas and many quotations in a studio he had concocted in his study. I was quite used to teaching dyslexics, but even so I sometimes came unstuck as I aimed to read and understand what he meant to say, rather than what was actually written! All three people, and our visiting lecturers, made for a fascinating three years, both of contextual theology and also our ministerial formation.

And so we arrived at the point of being ordained as deacons. We were now in a new group, so this was quite a transition. Being in the Chelmsford Diocese I was together with others in the same diocese, and we had all come from different traditions and colleges, some of whom were not used to being with others whose theology and practice of worship differed from their own. Once again I was very thankful for the diversity of our training, where differences had become opportunities for the whole of the previous three years. And not only was I still continuing my final year prison placement, and teaching, but I also became a curate in the centre of Southend, at St John's.

St John's was surrounded by car parks, where terraced streets had been demolished. We were in the middle of club land, with the Rossi ice cream factory jammed up against the church sanctuary, and the bus station just up the road. Homeless people slept in the churchyard, sharps and broken glass littered the site, and next door to the church was the huge Palace Hotel which looked out over the pier and the sea. At the time it housed asylum seekers. The nearby York Road was listed as the most dangerous in the area, in view of murders, arson and so on. Since I was teaching at the pupil referral unit, and working at the prison, and writing, the parish of Southend felt perfect, and I loved it.

My pastoral work happened in mainly two places. At the Palace Hotel I introduced myself and would walk around the 'streets' which were the hotel corridors, where mothers sat on the floor knitting and chatting while the children played. Soon we made friends and I often got invited into their 'homes', where whole families lived in a double bedroom. The wardrobe was usually jammed against the sea view window because of the freezing draughts coming in. I doubt any maintenance had been carried out. Communal bathrooms were off the main corridor and there was nothing movable in them. The kitchen was several floors down. Two double beds were squashed into each room, filling the space. And this was home. When cooking downstairs, the parent had to lock the children in the room for their safety, and to enjoy the delicious food they would spread a plastic tablecloth on the beds and we would sit on the beds to eat.

St John's and the Palace Hotel

On Saturday mornings I would walk the corridors playing my recorder, and soon had a trail of children behind me. We all made our way down to the hotel lobby where I had set up activities and bible teaching, linked to the next day. Some of the parents would come as well, and most were Christian at that time, so it worked well. On Sunday I would call at the hotel and bring anyone to church who wanted to come.

My other main ministerial outreach involved sitting at a table outside the church doors, with two chairs and two bibles. I sat there, praying and reading, and a steady stream of people would come and sit down for a chat, ask questions, pour out their sorrows, or pick their favourite bible passages. They weren't all Christian. Coachloads of trippers would have been set down at one of the car parks, and they would stop off at the church on their way to or from the town or beach. I always kept the church door open, and people would ask if they could sit inside. Sometimes Muslims and atheists would tell me it was the first time they had been in a church. By the evening the footfall was the young ones walking past on their way to a nightclub, and they sometimes stopped to chat.

Whenever we had food at a church activity I would take some round to those who lived in the churchyard, and several times I ended up taking their funerals, as we had become friends. So much unresolved grief and guilt. So much institutional inequality. Yet so much resilience in the human spirit. We are truly made in the likeness of God. All of us.

CHAPTER 20

THE HOLY LAND

It was during my curacy at St John's that I was visiting the Holy Land. In 2000, while still a student and ordinand, I had walked from Nazareth to Bethlehem with a small group of eight, some of whom were Palestinian guides who had been refused guide permits by the Israeli government. We walked through the West Bank, would stop for lunch and a rest under the trees, and sleep under the stars, or in black tents with carpets, or on the floor of people's homes. Always there was good conversation, a warm welcome, and excellent food, which we usually ate sitting round on the ground. Early starts meant early breakfasts – hot mint tea and freshly baked bread cooked on a fire.

If we were sleeping outside, the glaring orange lights on the hills reminded us of this being occupied land, with internationally illegal settlements and the clear unspoken message that we were not welcome. Our Palestinian companions would laugh sarcastically as they quoted the reason given for the orange lights, "This is for your security."

At the ancient limestone wells we could dip the bucket into an underground stream and haul up the refreshing 'living' (flowing) water to quench our thirst and pour over our heads. Along the route we would often come across wells which had been cemented up. This was a way of discouraging nomadic people from coming to the area, so the Israeli government could then say there was no one there, which they considered gave them permission to occupy the land and build their own settlements. Water was also being piped away from traditional watering places, resulting in Palestinian people having to buy their own water back from Israel.

One day we were hot and thirsty, looking forward to reaching a well which our guides said had not been cemented up. It was a shock when we got there to find the mud around the well still freshly imprinted with animal footprints, but the well itself recently blocked. I asked why the Palestinians didn't just unblock these illegally closed wells? They explained quietly that if this was done the wells would be blown up, and irreparably damaged. They preferred to save the wells from that.

It was heartbreaking to experience occupation and the terrible hardships suffered as a result. In one Bethlehem ruined house which had just been bombed by the Israeli army who we could see through the holes in the walls, the owner wept as he stood in his destroyed home. We queued at the checkpoints with people who held letters for hospital appointments, but were turned back, sick or bleeding. And we saw students running over the hills to get to college, risking being shot.

I want to make it clear that when I tell the uncomfortable truth about the practice and effects of Israeli occupation, I am not being anti-Semitic. I could sense the Israeli fear and know that our fear often leads us into particular actions. Nor am I talking about the Jewish people, many of whom were uncomfortable with the government's policies, and found the illegal occupation, the house demolitions and the wall building unnecessary or even abhorrent, and were doing all they could to protect people and raise awareness internationally. Sadly even today, giving a voice both to the Jewish and to the Palestinian people (who are of course, also Semitic) is viewed as anti-Semitism. As a member of Amnesty International I was sure, then as now, that part of our faith must be calling to account any governmental actions which result in human suffering such as is the case in the land we call Holy. No doubt there are many of you who would disagree, but my visits to

Israel and Palestine, and what I saw and experienced, did influence my faith journey.

On my visits I was reminded that Jesus was born in Bethlehem, and standing in the empty cave of his birth, with young armed teenage soldiers outside in the Square, I remembered that in his time also this land was occupied with soldiers everywhere. Only the names have changed. In Jerusalem I watched one of these young soldiers kicking a woman who was selling her vegetables. The vegetables went flying. The woman calmly gathered them and sat down again. The soldiers were young and confident, and their insults and aggressive behaviour were returned with dignity.

This was a dignified response I was shocked to find that I recognised in myself. Whether an abusive relationship is hidden in domestic situations, resulting in prison sentences, or part of normal life in racist State policy, dignity is often our only way of safely retaliating. And of course aggressive abuse of others is a classic example of what can happen when we are abused victims as children. Victims can become perpetrators, yet the truth is that they are still also victims. We who abused the Jewish people for so long, and particularly in the terrible atrocity of the Holocaust are in many ways the cause of what has now matured into the Israeli government's attitude to their Palestinian neighbours. History has dealt both nations such cruelties that it is impossible to untangle victims and perpetrators.

"How can we help?" I asked a grieving mother whose son had been killed. She answered, "please tell our story".

We were once staying in a village where an olive farmer was extracting the clear oil. Down the road the wall separated these farmers from their trees, and at random, unpublicised times, a group of soldiers would open the gate for them to go through. If they missed this brief opening, they had to leave the trees without harvesting the crop, and sometimes there was a deliberate shutting of the wall at harvest time. I also noticed that the water tanks on the top of houses had patched up shot holes. They told me that when these tanks were filled with precious water, soldiers would ride through the village taking potshots at the tanks so that the water would trickle out into the dust. We were introduced to Yasser Arafat on one visit. The next time I was there the whole building was a heap of rubble.

On one visit we were joining an attempt to walk from Bethlehem into Jerusalem, a short journey, but an impossible one for many, even when family members live in another part of this imprisoned land. Faith leaders led the way, and I was holding hands on one side with a Jewish woman and on the other side with a Muslim woman. I was there in the middle, a Christian priest, and we were all hoping that the presence of internationals might prevent bloodshed on this completely peaceful request. We carried olive branches of peace, and made our way through Bethlehem to the outskirts, where the Israeli tanks blocked our path. Armed soldiers sat on the tanks, taking videos of us, so we knew we were being noticed and marked.

Archbishop Riah of Jerusalem approached the military and politely requested that we could be allowed to walk into Jerusalem. We waited in silence, praying. I was looking straight into the barrel of a gun mounted on a tank, knowing that this quietness could explode into violence at any moment. I don't remember feeling frightened. In fact I was calm and ready for whatever might happen, because it felt exactly the right place to be, holding hands with my two companions, protecting them as best I could by my presence. And longing, as we all were, for a just and healing peace in this wounded Holy Land.

I think our presence did prevent those guns being fired, and the tear gas we were anticipating, for the time being, but we also knew that the army would wait until we internationals had left. With awful irony, we internationals were free to enter Jerusalem while those with more valid reasons for the journey, were not.

We were asked by them to be their representatives, which we did, continuing the journey and gathering in Jerusalem, where soldiers stood guard.

That evening – New Year's Eve – we found ourselves with other Europeans in Ramallah, joining the local inhabitants, where the streets were crammed and my feet barely touched the ground. As this river of people washed past the shot-marked and destroyed buildings, candles were handed back over heads, hand to hand, and lit with cigarette lighters. In the darkness we became a river of light as we approached the New Year, surging through the town to protest against the injustice and breaking of international law, and voicing our longing for a just peace.

On our return to the UK, using the Tel Aviv airport which, though open to us, was closed to residents on the wrong side of the wall, we were separated and questioned at length, our luggage scrutinised. At least I was ready to tell their story when I got home, as I had been asked.

This did result in hate mail, and accusations of being anti-Semitic. I was quite regularly shouted down and vilified. But there were also those who listened and subsequently went for themselves. I became good friends with an elderly Jewish man who sought me out to tell me he had lived in Israel and agreed with what I was saying. His name is Harold, and he played chess at a community café every week with a Muslim friend of his.

The good news is that there have been some amazingly courageous people who have worked with steadfast endeavour across the divides, refusing to be silenced. People like the group against house demolitions, the group of bereaved parents, the sport and music enterprises, the international accompaniers, all of whom hold the door open for progress to peace and mutual respect. Walls never last for ever, however strongly they are built, and I pray that these walls will one day be no longer in place. No longer considered necessary.

In 2003 the huge demonstration against the possibility of war with Iraq was held all over the world. Millions flocked to city centres to protest 'Not in my name'. I remember our walk through London, and the great gathering in Hyde Park. Surely such an outpouring of passionate feeling by so many would prevent our involvement in such a war? My local paper wanted to interview me at church about this, and I was happy to have the opportunity to explain why we were there. They pictured me holding a 'Not in my name' placard. Rather than taking notice of why we had protested, I was pilloried for holding a Muslim-produced banner in a Christian church!

Later I was due to be going on a visit to Jordan, and was already packed and ready to start my journey that day, when all the airports were shut down. The Iraq war had begun. I decided to go to London anyway, joining the prayers for peace, in St Paul's Cathedral and Westminster Abbey. It felt like the least I could do. Poor world. So often we reject love, listening and negotiating, and choose instead violence, hatred and war, in which no one ever wins.

CHAPTER 21

PRIESTLY MINISTRY

The time came for me to be ordained a priest. As I knelt and was surrounded by everyone's prayer, I remembered that Cursillo weekend in South Africa, when I had drawn this very time on an acetate over five years before. It was such a strange and extraordinary experience. The many hands didn't touch my head, and yet I felt a weight that propelled me far back in time to the early church, and then swung me back to the present, where I emerged as if from water, as a different species. It was unlike anything I had previously encountered. There was great joy in me as I emerged, and a tranquility or peacefulness of having been accepted and transformed into the Susan that God wanted me to be, exercising the ministry I was meant for, at this particular time.

I knew in a fresh way that I was to be a wounded healer, not as a good and holy person, but as a forgiven sinner. It was as if all my life experience up to then had been somehow a preparation for a priestly ministry. While at college we students had puzzled over why so many of us had emerged from places of wounding, and now it occurred to me that God, knowing the needs of his beloved people, had drawn us into priestly ministry precisely for such a time as this, a time we didn't yet know about. All we had done was give God, as it were, a blank cheque. Whatever the cost, we were happy to accept God's touch on our lives, if this was the way for God's will to be done on earth.

My curacy in the Southend Parish continued, though with a different flavour. My teaching in the pupil referral unit continued, with unexpectedly deep conversations arising from my wearing the clerical collar! My work as a prison chaplain continued, as I have explained. My writing continued, my visits to other communities around the world continued, and of course, my family continued, and I was now a Grandma as well as a mother.

As my curacy came to an end, Stephen Burdett, my very patient training incumbent(mentor), suggested the possibility of my becoming a team vicar in the team, based at St Mark's, which had been without a vicar for some time. At this point I want to tell you a bit about the Southend Parish. It was one parish in the centre of Southend, made up of four churches, though of course our remit was to be there for all those living and working in our area. This included Southend pier and the lifeboat station, Southend high street, with a train station at either end, several schools, the Cliffs Pavilion, the Adventure playground and the Southend seafront. It also included the many homeless and mentally ill who were often housed in former seaside boarding houses, all the day trippers and clubbers, together with the agencies which were addressing some of the needs in our area.

In this tidal community we were to be a steadfast and dedicated sign of God's kingdom. Churches are not commissioned to maintain the comfort of the congregation, but to equip the congregation to be church wherever their lives reach. Most of what is truly church goes on when the building is mainly empty. But the people are full. Full of God's grace and love which spills out in their every conversation and choice and financial investment. And if that isn't happening, then I can't see how we are being the Body of Christ.

I had become involved with the BarNBus project, which was an ecumenical outreach, responding to the many young people on the seafront. Using an old double decker bus, lovingly refurbished, we trained young volunteers, who each had another person praying for them and the bus whenever they were on duty. The bus would park up on the seafront, available and ready. Young people would come aboard, where they could get free hot drinks and snacks, and where there were people to chat with, a prayer room and a telly. We prayed beforehand and afterwards, and the police found that crime rates reduced whenever the bus was there. Before long there were other buses, parked in different areas.

The other significant event of this time, as I ended my curacy and began as team vicar, was that while my friend Christine and I were staying somewhere wild and beautiful in west Ireland, I decided to write to my husband who was living in Singapore. We had been separated for sixteen years now and I asked him if he would ever like us to get together again. He replied to my letter declining that possibility.

So I decided that perhaps the time had come for us to divorce. As you know, I had made those marriage vows in God's presence and when the divorce came, and I was granted decree nisi, I went and sat on the beach and wept. This was not how I had ever thought our marriage would end. That evening our ministry team was having a Christmas meal out, and I told them. They were all very kind, and made it easier. I remember we drank to the future!

As St Mark's had been without a vicar for some time, all of us in the Southend Team took it in turns to lead worship there and chair their church council meetings. The church is next to the busy C2C railway line between Shoeburyness and Tilbury and Fenchurch Street. It was built on the unfashionable north side of the tracks, with streets of small cottage terraces surrounding it. There had been a windmill built almost opposite, replacing a water mill on what are now mudflats below the Cliffs Pavilion. A forge was still working next door, mainly crafting wrought iron gates and fences.

Outside St Marks

The terraced houses were often multi tenanted, so the population was constantly changing. Politically the church was in Milton Ward, one of the most deprived wards in the country, yet situated just across the railway from the wealthy, gracefully built conservation area. St Mark's had started out as an iron church belonging to an Anglican clergyman, been sold to the Baptists who built a brick tabernacle, complete with a full immersion baptistry, and subsequently sold back to the Church of England, who built a balcony with foundation pillars set into the baptistry, and a sanctuary at what had been the back entrance. This meant the front of the church was now at the east end.

There were only ten or occasionally twelve people left in the congregation, all faithful and prayerful, who had managed to keep the church open against all the odds. I don't think they were overjoyed to have me appointed as team vicar because I would be sharing my time between the church, the prison and my writing, while they had been hoping for someone full time. Sadly for them, that wasn't really viable.

Yet when I arrived the pews had all been stacked up at the back, and the whole congregation were busily engaged in cleaning, painting and sanding down wood, in readiness for some new carpet. How often do we get 100% of a church community so actively engaged? I was very impressed, especially when tea and cake appeared. Such lovely, welcoming people, so steadfast and willing to work for the outreach and mission of their church. I got stuck in with them. I am sure it was largely due to their faith and prayer, and their enthusiasm, that the church began to grow.

The Milton Community Partnership was based at St Mark's hall, and we engaged the offenders team, who had been given community service rather than prison sentences, to paint and repair the hall. I became a trustee of the Milton Partnership so as to cement the link with the church. Jointly we ran a baby and toddler group, a family's programme, and a jacket potato club. The women's refuge held support meetings in the church, and university students came to the hall for their dance and drama classes. Outside became a community garden, with flowers and shrubs on the south side and vegetables and fruit on the east side. We installed solar panels, and switched to a sustainable energy supplier.

Soon the carpet in the church was laid, and the space at the back was filled with buggies and wheelchairs during services, because over a third of the congregation were now children. Others were wheeled from local care homes, and some were recovering and recovered gamblers from GA who were happy to find that St Mark's was a kind of 'God's living room!' The congregation reflected the worldwide community living and working near the church. A Zimbabwean pastor asked to rent the church for worship, and we worked it so that they arrived at coffee time. This meant that the two congregations could meet. Sometimes the Zimbabwean people would come early and join us for worship, and sometimes our members would stay on after coffee to enjoy their worship. In the end we all felt like one community and often worshipped together, linking St Mark's with Zimbabwe through gifts of items requested by the people and delivered by trusted friends.

It worked well, partly because most of the new church members had no preconceived ideas about what church should be, and the original members were always welcoming and accepting of newcomers. It was a happy time.

This is a poem I wrote at the time:

> The angels always love it
> When the toddlers start to pray.
> Toddlers know God likes the bells
> Shook hard, the toddler way,
> The alleluia's danced with friends
> And streamers waved to tangles.
> They know you need to see the world
> From many different angles.
> And after all the energetic praising has been done
> And candles have been lit and given out to everyone
> The toddlers and their angels,
> Sitting quietly side by side,
> Are contentedly at home,
> with all of heaven opened wide.

Before long I had decided it was impossible to continue at the prison as well, so I was down to two jobs which was more manageable.

CHAPTER 22

SURPRISE CHANGES

While I was at St John's I had started a parish bible study, and two men there were very kind and protective of me. They never left me at church on my own, and wouldn't go until they had seen me to my car. I had acquired a stalker, so this was actually very necessary. The bible study continued when I went to St Mark's, and at first we met in the church. Unfortunately my stalker made this unsafe, so we met instead at someone's home. John Hill, one of my two friends who had helped me at St John's, had fallen on hard times financially and I was concerned that he wasn't eating properly. At that time I was still at the prison, and the new incoming chaplain was living with me for part of the week. So my bible study friend would come and share a meal with us sometimes. He was especially fond of puddings.

Upstairs my family had moved to a house of their own, and the Lukas boys were living there each summer. So who were the Lukas boys? They had turned up at St Mark's one evening as I was leaving the church, asking if I knew of anywhere they could rent, as their landlord had decided to sell the house. They were from the Czech Republic and were students who had come for the summer holiday and had got jobs as refuse collectors. I said they could rent my upstairs if they liked, so they did. In fact they returned with yet more Lukas's for the next couple of years, an arrangement which suited us all. We are still in touch and I have an open invitation to stay with them. I presume there are some people in that country who are not called Lukas!

My bible study friend John Hill had started working for Milton Community partnership, and as he was there in the office each day, he had quite a ministry with people coming in for a chat. Annie, the new prison chaplain, was settling in well. My stalker, who was schizophrenic and needed far more care than he was getting, had become quite a serious threat to my safety, and when things came to a head in and out of church, and I was receiving regular death threats, my church wardens contacted the police. After a court case he was sentenced, and that was a relief. He was finally getting the help he needed, and the congregation and I were safe.

Then I got letters to say that my mortgage insurance would have a £5000 shortfall. This meant that I would have to move from Leigh. I sold the house in 2006, and although I had told both Annie and the Czech students, they didn't move out until the day before I moved out! I had nowhere to move to, but my sister Margaret, who nursed nights at the local hospice, was chatting to a colleague about my situation. This nurse was a nun, and said of course I should come and stay with them at the convent. So that's how I came to spend six happy months with sister Mercy, sister Kate and sister Liamie.

Most of my possessions were in storage, till I had found a place to live, and those lovely nuns gave me a nice room, with a bed, table and an armchair. I could use the kitchen, there was a well stocked library, and I could join the sisters for silent prayer each day. Often we'd end up chatting in their living room. I loved their company, and their way of life, and I wrote a book while I was there. It's called *Follow that Star* and explores the connection between the creation and the incarnation. I made good use of the library and our conversations.

During the time I was there, I would get some healthy sandwiches after church on a Sunday and call for John Hill at the property where he was renting a room. We'd sit at one of the beach shelters and eat our lunch looking out at the sea. I noticed he was often in pain, though he never mentioned it. He did say the doctor thought his shoulders ached a bit because of rheumatism, but the pain got worse.

By March 2007 I had bought a house in Southend and moved in. Part of the families project at MCP was arranging days out for families during the holidays, and John had come on one of these outings, as part of his work at MCP. On the coach he had a phone call from the hospital. Apparently they had decided he should have a blood test and it was showing a high reading for his PSA. He was to go to the hospital that week. By now the pain was making it hard for him to walk, and he couldn't manage driving. So I drove him to the hospital and had to get a wheelchair for him so he could make it into the cancer clinic.

As soon as he arrived it was all systems go. They gave him quite a brief examination and took him off to a ward straight away, with me running along behind them. Apparently your PSA shouldn't be higher than 8. John's was over 2000! The nurse told him he was a record breaker, but the other news wasn't so cheerful. John had prostate cancer which had already spread into his bones. That's why his shoulders had become so painful. It was an aggressive cancer, they said, and it was terminal. They could ease the pain by giving him hormone therapy and radiotherapy, but they thought he would be needing a care home, as his upstairs rented room, with shared bathroom and kitchen, wouldn't be suitable for his needs. He could last two years at the very most. It might well be far less.

John's children came and visited their Dad, and the doctor explained to them what the care plan was. John was courageous and accepting as ever, but obviously concerned. I suggested him moving to my new home, rather than a care home. It had an upstairs and a downstairs bathroom. We talked it over and agreed this might be best. So once John was out of hospital that's what happened. We got a stairlift. The occupational therapist organised handrails, a special chair and all kinds of useful equipment.

The hospital had put him on steroids so he could move better for a while, and I went with him to clear his room. His entire possessions were in two suitcases. A Macmillan nurse came round and was so supportive and helpful. John and I had become very fond of one another over the time we had known each other, prayed together and studied the bible together, and our friendship had become love. The following June 2008 we got married.

CHAPTER 23

MARRIAGE NUMBER 3

This wedding was packed with people, and full of joy. We were married at St John's, our dear friends Rae and Geoff drove me to church and my brother gave me away. Between us we already had plenty of grandchildren, and they were all in the wedding party. Lucky and his friend sang Zimbabwean songs, and the sun shone. Afterwards we all walked along overlooking the sea to the Cliffs Pavilion for a lovely meal and dancing.

Two days later we went to Tilbury, boarded the *Marco Polo*, and found a huge arrangement of flowers in our cabin from the lovely people at St Mark's. Our Macmillan nurse had carefully tweaked John's medication so he would be able to manage this trip.

Neither of us had thought we would ever marry again, and we were both amazed to discover that we could do marriage after all. John and I had met through praying together, and our marriage was like God's beautiful gift to us.

We had one wedding anniversary together and he died before our second. Our time together was so short, but so very happy. During that time we stayed with his parents and his brother and sister in law in Namibia, visited Venice by train, and even managed a short break in Derby only a month before he died. A truly remarkable man, and so very kind.

Do you remember how I felt my Mum had taught me how to be a deacon, through her love and her practical need? Well, my husband John taught me much about dying as he travelled this journey with such cheerful courage, grace and faith. It was an honour and a privilege to be with him on the journey.

There is so much I could say about our relationship which was lived out in God's company, but I don't think I'm up for that yet. I did keep a journal, and there were so many kindnesses from family, friends, and all those who had come to love John through Milton Community, and the church community. He was one of those rare people who never set out to be liked but end up being loved.

Once again, at his funeral, St John's was packed. Some had even come from Nigeria to be there, and I was told the bell was rung at the Lagos motorboat club as a tribute to him. Those who had only met him at Southend were amazed to hear about his previous life in Africa and all over the world. Those who had only known him poor were amazed to hear about his former wealth. I remember one of our friends saying how he so appreciated her biscuits, "and now I realise he must have eaten the very best of biscuits!" John was content with whatever happened. He still read his tattered bible every day, and his favourite Psalm was 103, the first verse of which is close to my heart as well:

> 'Bless the Lord, O my soul,
> And all that is within me bless his holy name.'

He also loved this hymn, which we had both at our wedding and his funeral:

> 'Praise my soul the King of heaven!
> To his feet thy tribute bring;
> Ransomed, healed, restored, forgiven,
> Who like me his praise should sing?
> Praise him, praise him, praise him, praise him
> Praise the everlasting King.'

The verse he specially loved was this:

> 'Fatherlike he tends and spares us.
> Well our feeble frame he knows.
> In his hands he gently bears us,
> Rescues us from all our foes.
> Praise him, praise him, praise him, praise him,
> **Widely as his mercy flows.'**

I have a picture of John in my hall so he is always there to greet me whenever I come in! God bless him.

Grieving is hard work, especially when all those in your place of work are also grieving. When other loved parishioners had died, it had been my privilege to help everyone through the grieving. With John's death I was split in two. My own grieving happened in secret, and the public grieving had to be tightly controlled. I found it made me incredibly tired.

I was very thankful that John had died at a time of year when I could walk and walk in the evenings until I could bring myself to come home. And even if we know all the stages of grief, that in no way means we can fast track the process. There is only one good way to grieve, and that is to grieve honestly, allowing it to take as long as it needs to take.

On the day he died, and all that week, it was wonderful to be surrounded by my African family and friends, so we could laugh and cry, remember and talk, without me being expected to do any entertaining. Food and drink just seemed to arrive, and I found this communal grieving incredibly precious. It makes me wonder if we have culturally shut out such valuable grieving, rather as we have shut ourselves off from the rest of the natural world.

On the first anniversary of his death I very definitely wanted to be somewhere else, so joined a pilgrimage to Jordan and Egypt. It felt right and good to remember John at Communion in Egypt in company with the other pilgrims, and it was also good to have finally made it to Jordan after my frustrated attempt before.

Partly because of the poignancy of this anniversary and partly because I had always longed to climb mount Sinai, our trek up this holy mountain was another cairn on my journey of faith. We started at midnight so as to reach the summit at sunrise. With the help of phones and torches, and accompanied for the first section by camels, we were a mixed group of people, some Jewish, some Muslim and some Christian. As we climbed higher the path got narrower and since this place is holy for all three faiths, it was such a joy and an honour to be sharing it with one another. Sometimes singing would happen. Different languages and faiths, but a real sense of unity.

The summit was rocky, more of a climb than a walk, and there was the sun rising, lighting up the landscape so beautifully, as we all praised God.

CHAPTER 24

AT A STROKE

I continued as Team vicar at St Mark's for another two years until I was due to retire at the beginning of July 2012. In our team meetings we planned my last service, and everything was settled and looking fine. But a few days before retirement day, on what would have been our second wedding anniversary, I woke up unable to focus. When I tried to get up it felt as if I was lurching along in a fast train. I thought this must be something to do with my eyes. I didn't realise, but I was having a stroke. Eventually I ended up in hospital.

I couldn't really believe this, but the MRI confirmed there was a clot. It was located in the cerebellum, so it didn't look like a classic stroke. Instead, all my coordination was affected, physically and mentally. I spent two weeks in the hospital at Southend, and two weeks at Burrswood hospital, where my friend Christine was chaplain. Both hospitals were wonderful, and helped me as much as they could. My granddaughter Miriam, who was then nine, has told me she wanted to test me out, once they were able to visit, so she asked me whether I thought a ladybird was black with red spots or red with black spots. Apparently I said, "What's a ladybird?" I wasn't very able in brain or body! I had to learn again to walk, talk, think, draw, write, read, and so on, without jerking all over the place. If I tried to wave I'd end up slapping my face. I slopped drinks if I tried to carry them, and had to get used to being wheeled around. All the retirement cards were superseded by the Get Well Soon cards.

At Southend hospital I was distraught at not being able to say goodbye to the parish, and begged them to let me out for the final service at least. They finally agreed, provided some friends wheeled me in after the service had started and wheeled me straight back to hospital before the service ended! Those wonderful friends, Rae and Geoff, agreed to take responsibility, and it happened.

I have absolutely no memory of it at all. Much later I was admiring a beautiful painting of the church and was told I had been given it that day, and had even smiled to say thank you. But I don't remember. At least everyone was able to say goodbye, even if I don't remember!

After four weeks in hospital I was given six weeks of carers coming in three times a day, and they also helped with my continuing physio. I was absolutely dedicated to the exercises and determined to make new brain pathways where my old ones were now blocked. The physios asked me what I would really like as my next goal. I said I wanted to get to the bus stop. My physio nodded and smiled. "How about getting to the front door?" she suggested.

Bit by bit, though, I did manage to control my brain and body again. And finally we did make it to the nearby bus stop. I was only able just to sit there for a while; getting on a bus was a whole new challenge.

My first real outing was when my family wheeled me to the Paralympics at Stratford in September. I was so excited, and the stewards were amazing. While my family went off to the seats we had booked long before my stroke, the stewards took me to a brilliant seat next to the Olympic flame, and there was a chair next to my wheelchair for my carer. So my sons-in-law would take it in turn to come and sit with me, along with their youngest children, who were convinced Grandma was about to take part as I was in a wheelchair like many of the athletes! I still couldn't clap, but I could certainly cheer. It was a glorious day and a huge milestone on my journey of recovery.

So what of my life pilgrimage – my journey of faith through these turbulent and life changing years?

There were times when I cried out to God like the psalmists. There were times when I was so wracked with grief that I couldn't pray, but others surrounded me and assured me of their prayers. There were times I forgot any prayers I started. This, I am certain, is why our prayers for others are so vital. We are, after all, the body of Christ, and just as when we break a leg the body doesn't die, but can't physically move properly for a while, so when any of us are crushed and broken emotionally or through serious physical illness, the rest of the body of Christ prays and holds that person in God's love. It is effective and I have experienced its efficacy. Basically we do what we can and not what we can't! But as church we are a working community of love, enabled and filled by God's love. Our task of care for one another involves a simple job of praying for one another. This includes not only our family and friends, but also those we are shown on the news, and those we meet or notice, on the bus or sitting outside a shop.

Sometimes this constant prayer will spur us into loving action. Sometimes the action is for others to carry out and our job is to support their action with our loving prayer. I suspect that when we die, we will no doubt see all the consequences of opportunities for kindness that we have missed. But also we will see the consequences of our loving prayers for others, even though we never knew this while we were bound in this temporal zone of earthly life. And that is truly humbling and a great joy.

Another thing I understood was that God surprises us so often, hearing the cry of our hearts, even when we haven't requested something. When I was a theology student one of my friends was the lovely secretary there, called Mary. I was, of course, a single parent at the time, certain that marriage was something I failed at with all guns blazing! She wanted me to ask God for a husband, but I laughed. There was no way I would ever marry again, and that was the last thing I would pray for. However, she said that she would pray, anyway, and God could always say "no" if it wasn't right. Well, Mary came to our wedding, and caught my eye as we walked down the aisle. We both smiled. God knows the longings of our hearts, whether we choose to voice them to ourselves or not.

And when I was catapulted into premature old age at a stroke, I found it incredibly frustrating of course, but I also learnt something I had heard from early childhood in my Dad's 'armchair'. It was those last words of Milton's poem 'On his blindness'.

'… they also serve who only stand and wait.'

My enforced dependence taught me more about what it really means to relinquish power and control. It is so easy to think we have mastered this when actually we haven't even come close to the sacrificial love Jesus demonstrates and asks us to share. All we do is play clever games so as to continue our love of power and subtle manipulation. There is a Franciscan story that shows this rather well.

Saint Francis was talking with brother Leo about what perfect joy isn't. Finally Leo begs Francis to say what perfect joy is! His answer is not what we might expect. Francis says that, for instance, if we were to have struggled through freezing ice and snow as it's getting dark, and eventually reach a house where we expect to find a warm welcome, but instead are thrown out, rejected and insulted… if we can manage even this without reacting in anger and indignation, but blessing, then THAT is perfect joy.

I'm not suggesting that this is easy or quick. It isn't. But I do think Francis is right, and the stroke helped me to understand a little better, the thankful way of living which John had also shown me. When we say the end of the Lord's Prayer we acknowledge that the real holder of the kingdom, the power and the glory is not us, but God. As Jesus said to Pilate, when Pilate reminded Jesus that he had the power to release him, Jesus replied that Pilate's power was not very powerful at all in the great scheme of things. He said that Pilate would have no power if God had not given it to him.

I think Jesus was well aware of how perfect love could only be demonstrated by undergoing completely undeserved crucifixion to death, without that love turning to anger and resentment whatever was unjustly thrown at him. Pilate was simply part of the events leading to that necessary acting out of perfect love.

As the body of Christ, inbreathed by such Godly capacity for loving, we are commissioned to live in the same self emptying way. Sometimes even our life events which we find most difficult, can be our best teachers.

CHAPTER 25

THE ATLANTIC OCEAN

Slowly, with the support of excellent physio and stubborn determination in probably pushing myself too fast, I recovered. Owing to the stroke happening so soon before retiring, I found that retirement had disappeared from view, and in its place were the more pressing matters of disability and recovery. What I had been planning once I was retired was, believe it or not, a lengthy pilgrimage! I had thought I would step out of my home and walk back home, via the rest of the world. I wanted to worship with those living in mountains, valleys, deserts, forests and arctic wastes, crowded cities and isolated villages, among the very poor and the very wealthy. This was not likely to be possible now, but I could dream.

Then a chance conversation with Rae and Geoff shifted the impasse.

I had assumed that my state pension included my teaching pension. They didn't think this was right, and suggested I look into it, which I did. Surprisingly I discovered that not only was there a pension, but also a lump sum waiting to be claimed. The same day a leaflet came through my door advertising a month long cruise to the Amazon, starting and finishing at Tilbury. I phoned both my lovely daughters to ask what they thought. Would I be crazy to spend that lump sum on this cruise? Both of them said, "go for it Mum! You've always wanted to go to the Amazon, and you can use the ship as a means of doing that pilgrimage you planned." They know me well, bless them, and their encouragement decided me. The lump sum arrived one day and the next day I had booked a place. The *Marco Polo* would set sail mid January and be back by mid February.

I found some appropriate clothes in charity shops and it wasn't long before I was aboard. I knew the ship from when John and I had been on our honeymoon, so it was familiar, and I found a quiet place down near the water at the bow, where I would do morning and evening prayer. I kept a journal and loved getting to know the South and North Atlantic in all its different moods. I also led worship with a couple of other pastors, and was a kind of unofficial chaplain.

After going across to Amsterdam, where I spent a happy time in the Reichsmuseum, we sailed through the Bay of Biscay and docked at Lisbon before visiting Cape Verde, off the coast of Africa. Then came the crossing of the great Atlantic to Brazil where we hugged the coast and entered the Amazon river. Each day we sailed further up until we reached Manaus. And each day we disembarked to explore that fragile and beautiful rainforest.

From the Amazon we sailed north to Guyana, before visiting the windward islands of the Caribbean and then heading back across the North Atlantic via the Azores. By this time in February severe storms were threatened, and since these storms were coming in waves, (if you'll pardon the pun) our captain made the decision to continue on our way in case we got stuck in the Azores.

As we made our way through the churning Atlantic towards the English Channel, it was Valentine's Day, when huge storms were battering all the coast on both sides of the Channel. It was very tricky to walk on the ship and everything was sliding about loudly as I made my way downstairs to lunch in the dining room. I sat at a table near a window and was waiting to be served when I saw an enormous wave coming straight for us.

I thought it was going to break the window and come into the ship, and quite calmly found myself thinking that this, then, was how I was going to die.

As it happened the wave crashed through the next window instead of where I was sitting, and sadly the gentleman sitting at that next table to me was killed, though we didn't know this at the time. Another passenger was also badly wounded. We were all knocked back off our seats, some distance from the tables. The crew ran to block the window, where the raging water was pouring in, and we were holding on to each other in a line as we waded through water, broken glass and blood, on the pitching ship. Of course the storm was still raging, so it wasn't that easy to keep our balance, but the crew helped us all. We were led to an upstairs open area where we had to sit on the floor, wedging ourselves against the wall to stop ourselves sliding across the carpet. We were wet and rather shaky. The crew raided one of the nearby bars and handed us all crisps and chocolate, they brought us towels and we hugged each other.

The two severe casualties were to be airlifted to Brest, but for the helicopter to hover and the hoist to be lowered, the captain had to turn the ship 180 degrees. This meant going sideways to the huge waves, and I knew from my white water canoeing days that this was quite a dangerous manoeuvre. It took twenty minutes for us to get round into position and the first casualty was carried past where I was sitting on the floor. I remember thinking that he looked dead.

After quite a long time we heard and felt the helicopter flying away. We were told that they would be coming back for the other casualty. So we went through the whole procedure again. After hours had passed two crew members worked their way along the row of us, carefully taking us down to our cabins. They insisted on checking that everything was still in place there before letting us in, and telling us to stay put. The ship was still pitching and rocking, but I got on the bed and held on.

Not long after I was amazed to be brought some hot food! Those crew were incredible, and I am so thankful for all their help. It was another possible death experience though, and throughout I was pretty convinced that we might drown. I couldn't see how we would survive with all that water inside the ship.

I decided not to tell my family until I got home a couple of days later, as I was afraid they would worry. But our ship was on the television news so I contacted them to let them know I was fine. They, of course, were shocked to watch my ship which had been crashed into by a freak wave during the storms they were all experiencing, with the news that one passenger had died.

Next morning we were brought breakfast to our cabins, but later we were allowed out. The crew had put the ship to rights, apart from the dining area. The storm still raged but we were now more sheltered, as we had reached the English Channel. We sailed through the channel to the rough North Sea, then turned into the Thames and docked at Tilbury. Next morning we woke to sunshine and calm waters. It seemed extraordinary, almost magical, the difference in weather and water from the days before. It was hard to believe that what we had just been through had really happened. Of course there was a time when many ships came to grief in storms, and many were drowned. That experience gave me a real sense of getting to know the Atlantic Ocean, and increased my respect for it and those who work on it.

We only have to look at the shapes of Africa and America to see that we are not the only ones who journey. The very tectonic plates of our planet home slide and shift, and at one time there was no Atlantic. I gather that there will come a time when it closes up again.

I wrote this song while I got to know the ocean.

THE GREAT ATLANTIC

The great Atlantic slides around us,
Waves surround us
To the edges of the sky.
No matter which way I look.
A walk I took around the deck
Was just a walk around a speck
Inside the distance of an ocean
Gently breathing with the motion
As the great Atlantic slides around us.

> *Chorus*
> And even if we sailed here forever
> Maybe we'd never really get to understand
> All the water, time and space
> Awash within this ocean place
> And the dreams awash within us, and
> sleeping...
> Perhaps the ocean teaches us
> As its ancient music reaches us
> And awakes the dream inside us once again?
> And awakes the dream inside us, once again.

Watching the waves meandering
Mountains and caves entangling
Spilling their sun bleached lace from the crest
To the rest of the blue.
If only we knew!
Driven by streams deep beneath us
Just like our dreams deep within us
Urging us on...

Chorus

And even if we sailed here forever
Maybe we'd never really get to understand
All the water, time and space
Awash within this ocean place
And the dreams awash within us, and
sleeping...
Perhaps the ocean teaches us
As its ancient music reaches us
And awakes the dream inside us once again?
And awakes the dream inside us, once again.

CHAPTER 26

CHINGFORD

I continued recovering, building new brain pathways, adapting to different ways of managing normal life. And eventually I was able to walk with only a stick for support. At this point I started to realise I was retired in my priestly ministry, although I was beginning to take up writing again. I found myself asking God what I should do now that I was recovered probably as much as I would ever be. During those four years I'd rested, certainly, so now I could feel I had itchy feet!

I unexpectedly saw an advert in the *Church Times* for a House For Duty post in Chingford, and I wondered if this might be a possible next move. Being London, there would be plenty of public transport, which I needed as I could no longer drive. It wasn't too far from Southend, so I could come home for a proper rest every week. And some of my family lived down the road at Walthamstow, so I wouldn't be miles from my support network. But most importantly, I would be able to minister again, if they were able and willing to have a stroke survivor!

So I contacted the rector for a preliminary chat, applied, and was overjoyed to be accepted. Just before starting I went on a week's retreat. There are two churches in the parish, and I was mainly at All Saints, usually known as the old church. It is a very beautiful, ancient church, on a hill overlooking the city, and the river Lea. Opposite is the open cemetery where the Kray brothers are buried. Full of prayer-soaked peace, this church was the perfect place to have come to. The people were welcoming and friendly, and I was so thankful to be here. I started in November 2016.

One morning in February I woke with a pain which I presumed would go away. It didn't. Instead it got worse. My GP said it was probably appendicitis and I was taken to Whipps Cross hospital. They gave me a CT scan prior to surgery and came to see me straight after this to tell me that it was actually bowel cancer, and I needed emergency surgery.

That was a surprise. I'd never needed any surgery before, and I hadn't had any signs of cancer. I didn't have long to worry, at least, I thought, while they assured me I would probably need a bag afterwards. I wondered if, as it seemed to be a bit serious, I might die from this. Oh well, I thought, if I do die from cancer at least I won't be getting dementia.

The operation process was quite an adventure as it was all new to me, and I was treated with such kindness and care. My daughter had arrived to be with me, and was still there when I eventually got wheeled up to the ward. The surgeons came cheerily in to say they'd managed to join me up so I wouldn't need a bag after all. And the cancer had already affected my appendix so they'd taken that out as well. A job lot, you might say.

After a couple of months I had recovered, and was back at work. By the beginning of July I was feeling fine, and we were booked on a diocesan conference held at Essex University. The campus was not great for people like me who couldn't manage stairs. My bedroom was on the third floor, in a building some distance from the main venue, and there didn't seem to be anywhere public to sit as we queued for food. Before the stroke I wouldn't even have noticed. Now, I found these details problematic. My rector, Andy, was so thoughtful, helping me wherever he could.

But I suppose it was all a bit too much, and I had another stroke. I just wanted to get home so refused hospital, which was probably stupid, but there you are! Father Andy found a wheelchair for me as I couldn't walk, Father Clive and Mother Cherry drove me back to Southend and somehow got me indoors. And I slept for England, expecting everything to get back to normal after a few days.

After a week or so I managed to get back to Chingford, but I wasn't really up to much, and couldn't do my job. I contacted my GP as I still wasn't able to do much, and he sent me to Whipps Cross again. They gave me various tests and decided that although they couldn't see new brain scarring, it had been a stroke, and I was put into the physio rehab programme, which I obviously needed. It was all a bit gloomy being back in this territory again, and I didn't find it easy to pray.

But I had taken in the kindest asylum seeker ever, to share my vicarage space, and he was truly wonderful. He cooked for us both, looked after me, and I helped him a little with his English. He was and is a wonderful friend and companion, a faithful Muslim, and we would sit and pray, with our two candles lit. I am so thankful for him.

It was taking a long time to learn walking again, and I was still trying to manage with my stick, which unbalanced me. One day I went into an AbleAid shop, rather desperate, and asked if they had anything which might help. They produced a walker and showed me how it would make walking less of an exhausting ordeal. So I bought it, there and then, and it did help. I could walk more upright, and it helped my balance.

By October I had begun to realise that, lovely as Chingford was, I could no longer do what I had been appointed for. Visiting parishioners, leading worship, taking funerals, weddings and baptisms, opening up the churches for morning and evening prayer... I simply couldn't do any of it now, so I came to the unwelcome conclusion that the kindest way forward was to resign, so that they could appoint someone able bodied. Andy and I talked it all over, and prayed together. We were both tearful.

CHAPTER 27

SOUTHEND AGAIN

So in January 2018 I moved back to Southend, confused and concerned. Had I got it wrong? I must have already had that cancer when I applied for the Chingford job. I didn't know. All I do know is that I sensed God's leading which brought me to Chingford. And now I just felt deeply sad, missed living in London, and still couldn't walk properly. But I did now have two Polish lodgers living in my spare rooms at Southend, and their company really helped. And I had family nearby, who once again were marvellous at noticing needs and being there to help. I got wheeled around wherever I couldn't use my walker, and Southend continued the physiotherapy. Bit by bit those new brain pathways got built, and although using a walker was still necessary, I could manage most things quite well.

I began to help out at St Clements, St Albans and St Andrews again, and joined a gym and the Mudlarks choir, which was a real joy each week. I completed my MA in Christian Spirituality, protested with XR in London, joined the Christian vigil in front of the Houses of Parliament, and wrote another book. As I recovered this time I felt it would be irresponsible to go for another House for Duty. In any case, I didn't really feel fit or able enough. It was time to embark on retirement. My friend Elizabeth and I would go for walks, and I started painting again.

One day in March 2020 I found my daily walk felt unusually exhausting, so I didn't go out the next couple of days. But then the Covid symptoms started in earnest. Like many others at this time, I didn't want to go to hospital if I could help it, because the NHS was inundated. 111 advised me to get to hospital but I felt too ill. As I worked through each breath I held my phone ready to contact 999, but I don't remember much about this time, only that I had never felt this ill before. Thankfully that time didn't last too long, only a couple of weeks, but I couldn't understand why the symptoms were still there for weeks and months afterwards. Breathing difficulties, total exhaustion and the hoarse voice seemed to be stuck.

This was now lockdown, of course, but I couldn't do much anyway, so spent most of my days either sleeping, or sitting still or lying down in the garden. I'd be there for hours, until the birds and insects got on with their lives as if I wasn't there. I couldn't think clearly enough to pray, but knew my stillness was a kind of prayer. In some ways this was a very special time, directing my feeble attention to what I wouldn't normally even notice. Like buds slowly opening into flowers, or spiders weaving a complete web, or solitary bees digging tunnels in stumps of wood.

One day I still felt so unwell I contacted the doctor, who could hear from my voice and breathing that all wasn't well. That afternoon my daughter had come round as usual to see how I was, and she thought I needed an ambulance. I wasn't so sure. "Look" I croaked, standing up, "I can stand up, I can't be that bad". That was when I had yet another stroke. It was different from before, with more classic symptoms, and I remember the paramedics asking me things, but my face wouldn't work and I couldn't answer. They blue-lighted me to hospital and thrombolised me, to disperse the clot. It was amazing how, in a matter of hours, I could talk and move again. They explained that I was going to the stroke unit and I asked if I could walk there. No, they said, it would be strict bedrest for a few days!

They were so kind in the hospital, and we patients made friends as well. This stroke reminded me of the one my Dad had suffered and I was very thankful for the way they had mended me. Out of this thankfulness grew a thought. I wanted to make a pilgrimage of Thanksgiving for Life. Not only my recovery, but even wider than that, I felt a huge thankfulness for this extraordinary and fragile gift of Life itself. As I rested and got stronger, that first thought grew into a plan. I would walk for a week, starting out from my local church of St Alban's, where I had first experienced God's holiness, and making my way to the city of St Alban's, where St Alban and the priest are laid to rest. It is still a place of pilgrimage for many.

And so this pilgrimage thought became a reality.

CHAPTER 28

THE PILGRIMAGE

Preparation

Jesus advises his would-be followers to do the maths! His stories of weighing up the opposing army before engaging in battle, or starting to build a tower and running out of money so the building ends up embarrassingly half built, are not only quite funny, but also very practical. Becoming a follower of Christ is a huge decision to make, and we do need to think hard before committing ourselves to something so drastically life changing.

For a walking pilgrimage, too, we need to plan and prepare, and this is all part of the journey. Quite a few people tried to dissuade me from undertaking my pilgrimage so soon after a stroke, when Covid was still rampant, even though the first lockdown had been lifted. Others who knew me well could see that I was going to do it anyway, so they encouraged me to do it as safely as possible. My family insisted I booked places to stay each night before I left home, and chose routes where I could use public transport if necessary. Together we worked out possible routes, based on the number of miles I could realistically expect to cover in a day.

I downloaded the Ordnance Survey maps on to my phone, (my Dad would be happy!) so I could always find where I was, even when I went wrong and lost my way. My family also gave me stacks of easy, nutritious snacks, so my blood sugar didn't drop too low. And of course I would be keeping in touch by messaging. Fr Neil, the vicar of St Albans, made contact with the Dean at St Alban's Cathedral, so they knew when I was planning to arrive. The usual time for our Eucharist at Westcliff was brought forward on the Saturday I was to leave, so that I could be blessed on my way and still have time to reach my first stopping place. They would all walk with me for the first stage.

As psalm 139 describes so wonderingly, babies also make preparations before they come to the point of birth, as God 'knits them together in the womb'. And Mary made that journey to her cousin Elizabeth early on in her pregnancy. We are told Elizabeth found that her baby 'leapt in her womb' when Mary, and the unborn Jesus, arrived. Joseph's preparations were different, but just as honest and necessary. He had to do a U-turn in his thinking, and often the hardest journey we ever make is that journey which takes place between our ears, as our thinking needs a drastic change of gear or direction. The word 'prejudice' describes the way we are so good at pre-judging, and that can so easily steer us off course, as I have often found in my own life journey. But once Joseph has been convinced, he is ready to do what God needs him to do, and this he does magnificently. Mary and the baby are protected from harm on the walk to Bethlehem and later, on their escape from Herod. They are in safe hands.

During the time of preparations things don't always work out as straightforwardly as you imagined. For me there were some expected difficulties and some I hadn't bargained for. Covid was obviously going to affect my route, as many places with overnight accommodation were closed. This meant trawling through the available places, choosing those near public transport. I ended up taking quite a zigzag route, dictated by Covid. I prayed my way through this research and planning, happy in the knowledge that God already knew and loved all my planned hosts, and was happy to arrange for me to turn up where God needed me to be!

A less expected problem turned out to be a lack of ways to cross over, or tunnel under the main roads and railways. I hadn't realised quite how much of our country is designed with cars and lorries in mind, rather than pedestrians. Sometimes this meant that I needed to alter my route considerably so as to access the only available crossing place. Narrow country lanes without pavements would be too dangerous for a disabled pilgrim with a walker, and some of the footpaths had so many stiles, or were so narrow and overgrown that these too were not possible for me. I also had to discount any bridges with steps, since I couldn't manage these, so route planning was quite a challenge, and involved finding and choosing only such options as were viable. Sometimes this felt like when, in a labyrinth, you seem to be going away from the centre, but actually this is what will eventually get you to the centre.

Even this planning stage of a pilgrimage reflects our life pilgrimage, doesn't it? Our first career or life plan may often need to be altered or compromised. Sometimes we do end up achieving an early longing – as I did eventually get to Africa – but it was a very circuitous route to reach it, and when I finally got there it was almost as if I had caught up with my original dream! And some our our dreams never materialise, for all kinds of reasons.

I don't buy into the commonly held conviction that 'everything happens for a reason'. This is not biblically grounded, and Jesus didn't teach it, so we perhaps need to question it, before accepting it as gospel.

What I am sure about, however, is that God's love is super steadfast and faithful, and whatever crazy routes we choose, God in humility and love is prepared to stay with us.

It's as if God is saying, "okay, so you're choosing this path? Not what I would have chosen for you, but let's do it together then. If we stick together, I'll be able to bring some blessing even from this!"

All through our lives we make choices, some of which are sensibly linked with God's will, while others are based on short term gains or self-centred wishes. Some are just foolish, or based on ignorance, but seemed a good idea at the time! Then there are those choices which are really gut reactions to some unhealed hurts we have experienced. Often we make our choices first, and then create our stories to justify them, to others, and even to ourselves.

This kind of planning and preparation doesn't just happen when we are young and inexperienced. Throughout our whole life pilgrimage that tangle of choices goes on. And Jesus is right: the more we learn to renounce self, and focus instead on becoming the loving person God knows will make us full of joy, the more we will be enabled to choose wisely, and be set free from the ghosts and chains that otherwise haunt our choice making.

Another part of my preparation was deciding what to pack. In our life pilgrimage we often struggle along, trying to carry the heavy weight of things we don't really need.

This may be seething anger over something that happened years ago, which we are still not prepared to discard. It may be the heavy effort of hiding long kept secrets, even from ourselves, so that we end up believing our own edited version, rather than acknowledging the reality, and setting down the long held false version. We may still carry cumbersome attitudes and prejudices which served our purpose once, but are no longer helpful.

So a pilgrimage reminds us, as we lighten our pack, of what we could also usefully dump to make our life pilgrimage easier, and happier. To become more like people of blessing.

Living simply is a challenge, but also a marvellous opportunity, not only physically and economically but also spiritually.

Day 1: Southend to Pitsea
Saturday 12 August 2020

So, I dressed in clerical uniform, with my Franciscan tee shirt over the top, and walking boots on my feet.

I was travelling as light as possible, partly because it was easier, and partly because I didn't want to be self reliant. Travelling very light meant that I would be forced to get food and shelter along the way. I didn't carry any placards because I wasn't campaigning this time, but simply walking in God's good company, content to arrive where I ended up, to use public transport whenever I needed to and talk with whoever I happened to meet. I felt that so much of our usual lifestyle is manipulative – sometimes necessarily so – but for this week, on a pilgrimage of Thanksgiving for Life, my agenda was to have no agenda, apart from journeying thankfully. I wanted to be reminded of my dependency on others and on God.

As I locked up and left my home, I prayed that it would be kept safe. Then I walked round to St Alban's, my nearest church. Even though this was a walk I did frequently, today on this sunny morning, it felt very exciting. Instead of being locked into a long and difficult stroke recovery, which I would have been if I hadn't been thrombolised, I felt overwhelmingly thankful that I was starting out on the pilgrimage I had dreamt of doing while in hospital. Colours seemed brighter, and I was noticing everything as if for the first time. I felt in company with other pilgrims throughout history and across the world, and in company with those embarking on their own faith journeys, as I had been when I walked the Penine Way after Ingleborough, as well as when I was a young child.

It was good to be starting out at church with the Eucharist, followed by the Franciscan blessing for those embarking on a journey. They let me lead the way out of church, out into God's world, out into the precious gift of life in all its fullness. We all walked together to the Thames, making our way past the Cliffs Pavilion and down the cliffs, so we could use the flat path beside the sea right into Old Leigh. There was a surprise waiting for us all at Chalkwell shelter. This is by the Crowstone, which marks the end of the Port of London Authority, and the start of the estuary. The Coast Guards and their volunteer helpers have a base here, as every year people get cut off by the fast, incoming tides, or swept out towards the North Sea on inflatables. One of our congregation, Maurice, had told them about the walk, and here they were, welcoming us with coffee and biscuits, socially distanced seating, and smiles. It was so kind and unexpected!

Suitably refreshed, we walked on to Old Leigh, which was crammed with visitors thankful to be out again after lockdown. Even the pubs were open. Here my lovely supportive church and family left, and two walkers from church continued with me to the café behind Leigh station, where we sat outside and enjoyed some lunch. Before long we were on our way again, walking on the wide path from Leigh to Benfleet station. I was beginning to get tired, and this path was rutted and uneven, so quite tricky to manage with a walker. But the grasses, cows and birdsong were lovely, and we could see Hadleigh castle over on the other side of the railway line. It was here that my busy sister managed to catch up with us and we walked together into Benfleet.

I used to live in Benfleet and the girls were born there, so it felt good to be here again on this first day. Memories of the antenatal clinic, the pub and the church were again like a life pilgrimage, when our present always references our past and informs our future. Here my sister and friends left. I had been so blessed with the send off and support, and now as I started across the recreation ground I felt the pilgrimage overture had been played. From now on I was on my own.

Almost immediately a dog walker stopped and we chatted. Further on two mums and their children were picking blackberries, and I checked the way with them. Another conversation and some helpful advice. They told me the path I needed had just been cleared, so I'd find it easier. And where was I going, they wanted to know. I wasn't sure whether to say St Alban's or Pitsea, but decided on Pitsea. When I reached the path we had talked about, I could see why they were glad it had been cleared. In fact, overgrown trees and nettles had been cut down, much of which was still lying there, so I couldn't have used the path unless this work had been done. As it was, I made very slow progress, lifting my walker over the tree stumps and branches, and stopping for breath every few steps.

And then suddenly the path opened out on to the churchyard of St Margaret's at Bowers Gifford. The evening sun lit up this ancient stone church, where I had once made a brass rubbing with a friend from school. Each time I'd taken the train to London I had looked out for this little church and enjoyed it. Now, for it to be suddenly there, still and quiet as I emerged from the difficult wooded path, it felt like a sanctuary, the perfect place to pray. So I had a rest, sitting on my walker, praying, eating a snack and drinking my water, before setting off to climb the hilly lane up to the A13.

I was joined by a group of men pushing their bikes, as one bike had a puncture, and they told me about their day's ride and the wildlife they had seen. Now they were waiting for one of the wives to come and collect them and their bikes. She soon arrived in a four-by-four, and we said our goodbyes. I trudged on up the hill, wondering how I was going to cross the A13 which was sounding louder as I got closer. I was very happy to find a narrow tunnel under the road, which hadn't shown on the map. It continued the direction of the lane I was on, and at the other side of the road became a lane again, so the recent A13 must have been built right across the old lane to the church. This lane led right up to what had been the old A13. It was like a landscape from the past still there in spite of the newer needs and road building.

When I had taught at Chalvedon in Pitsea, this older road was the only way home, and got snarled up with barely moving

traffic every rush hour. After work we would often stop off at the pub until later, when the road had cleared a bit. This was before breathalysing of course!

I now had to walk along a narrow, overgrown pavement as the traffic raced past. I could feel that I had overdone the walking today, but just focused on putting one foot in front of the other. Finally I reached Rectory Road and turned into it. Thankfully the pavement here was wider and the going easier. When I reached St Gabriel's church I sat down and contacted the Airbnb. My map showed it was close, but the road name wasn't there, and I didn't have the energy to make mistakes at this point. Loveness, my host, sounded friendly, very welcoming, and African, but didn't seem able to direct me, so I walked on, hoping to find the place soon. After several mistakes I happened on the street name. It was just a row of houses set back from Rectory Road. Spurred on I carried on, and joy of joys, arrived at the right number, where my lovely host opened the door wide and ushered me in.

She was taken aback by my walker and the distance I had covered, and was phoning her friend to say she couldn't now join in the prayer meeting as I had arrived. But I assured her I was very happy for her to take part in her online prayer meeting and she was thrilled that I was happy to join her. So we sat side by side in her gracious living room, like old friends, praying, partly in English, and I was invited to read one of the bible passages. The prayer group members all prayed for me. I hadn't even taken off my boots! It was a lovely African welcome to end my first day of pilgrimage. I couldn't have asked for anything better!

On our lifetime journey, too, there are times when we are loved and supported as we travel, and sometimes it is those unexpected kindnesses that buoy us up and remind us of how lovely people can be at their best. There are also times when we have to say goodbye, and carry on by ourselves. My Mum used to call such times 'little deaths' which sounds rather morbid, but I think she had a point. We do prepare for the big separations through these little ones, and Jesus's promise to be always with us holds true for the very difficult, sad and unsettling times as well as when all is going swimmingly.

And there are times in life when we thought we knew where we were going and suddenly we're lost. Maybe we even find no help where we hoped to find it. And what do we do then? Today, when I was tired and lost in Rectory Road, I recognised that, yes, there are times when we just have to go on anyway, and then we get there in the end. Giving up too soon isn't that helpful.

Day 2: Pitsea to Wyatt's Green
Sunday 13 September 2020

As part of my planning I had found a church which would be open after lockdown, and had a service at a good time for me. So after a good night's sleep and a good breakfast I crossed the road and waited in the morning sunlight for the bus that would take me to Basildon bus station. It was an interesting route, so I got to see quite a lot of Pitsea and Basildon. The town centre was full of complex roadworks which we negotiated before arriving at the bus station.

From here I walked across to St Martin's church, to find they were waiting outside to welcome me! I think my vicar had got in touch with them. It was so kind. I was shown to my socially distanced seat, and yes, they prayed for me. I felt I already had so much to be thankful for, and loved being able to join this worshipping community. After the service I walked to Basildon station, by a roundabout route dictated by the massive roadworks. On the platform I made friends with a family who were also waiting for the train. One great advantage of travelling alone is that you aren't alone for long!

You may well be wondering why I was taking such a curious route from Basildon, so I will explain. Today I would be making my way to a village north west of Brentwood, where my friends had kindly agreed to put me up for the night. In my preparation I had tried out all kinds of ways to get there, but it seemed impossible, bearing in mind the terrain I couldn't manage. Crossing the railway line and main roads was the problem. In the end, in desperation, I had contacted another friend who said her husband could meet me at the London bound side of West Horndon station. He would help me and my walker over the railway bridge, then drive me across the

A127, depositing me on the north side, so that I could walk through Thornton country park to Brentwood.

This sounds complicated I know, but that was the only way to do it... A bit like taking a sledgehammer to crack open a walnut! To get to West Horndon station I had to travel two stops from Basildon, and that's why I ended up chatting with a family on the platform at Basildon station.

Although it was only two stops, and hardly any distance, the ride to West Horndon felt like quite a trip as I looked out of the window and watched the summer trees beginning to change colour. At the station there was Phil, true to his word, and I was very happy to see him as there was no one else around, so I couldn't have managed without his assistance on this strange but necessary part of the journey. As we got into the car he handed me a lovely packed lunch which his wife Sue had made for me, perfect for a picnic in the country park. Phil and Sue are both very busy people on a Sunday, and I was so grateful for their help.

My map showed that I could go through the south and then the north parts of the country park, so first I found a lovely view and some trees for shade where I ate my picnic and made a recording for the diocese. It was turning into a very Franciscan sort of day.

Thorndon country park has woodland, with lakes and open spaces, and lots of wildlife. I was reminded of a poem I wrote once:

WOODS

See the great oaks' branches brandishing the sky;
Footsteps, leaf mould muted, where the acorns lie.
Just a thin, faint rattle as the last leaves die,
Meandering down yellow light, quite rusted, parchment dry.

A blackbird calls.

The silence, as he waits for a reply,
Sharpens years to moments,
And time to eternity.

I've always loved woodland!

The visitor centre is in the north section, and plenty of visitors come to enjoy this tamed, but still wild natural place. There were paths wide enough for me to use comfortably, and I knew I was heading north, away from the sun. The precise route was much harder to work out, so I just walked roughly in the right direction, following whichever paths seemed to lead the way I wanted to go.

Several times I asked people coming the other way, so as to check my route, and they were friendly and helpful. Even so, I found I had come out on to the A128 at Herongate. I knew I could simply follow the road up the hill into Brentwood – I had often driven up this road in my driving days. But the road was busy and noisy, and the trees of the country park beckoned, so I decided to make my way into the north section. This was easier thought than done. I saw a man with his dog emerge from the wood further up, so went to this opening. After a while the promising path narrowed and disappeared. So rather than wasting the way I'd already come, I pushed through the undergrowth and made my way to where I could see light beyond the trees.   I came out on to a golf course, and apologised to a couple of golfers who I had surprised. I explained that I was lost and could they please tell me how to get to the north part of Thorndon country park.

They pointed out a small building in the distance. Apparently that was their clubhouse, and they said I'd find the lane there. I thanked them and started on an uneven, difficult walk to the clubhouse. Eventually I got to the car park there, and asked some members who were getting out of their car how I could find the visitors' centre in the country park. They didn't really know but said there was a footpath off to the left from the road which probably went there.

This seemed the best I could do, so I found the footpath and set off. I think it had been fairly recently shut off from the golf course by a wire fence, so it reminded me of walking along beside the prison. A cyclist screeched to a halt as he hadn't expected to find a disabled pilgrim with a walker coming up the path!

It led to a junction of paths, one of which had a signpost to the visitors centre, so I turned up this path, full of hope, and happy to have found my way. Unfortunately it must have been an old sign, because it led to a newly erected wire fence, with a rather large and angry sign proclaiming that this was private land, and there was no thoroughfare.

So I was faced with a challenge. Should I walk all the way back to the junction and try another path? Or should I use the map and the sun to blaze a trail to where I could see I needed to get to?

I decided to choose the second option, and could see that others had done the same. I negotiated deep ditches, tangled undergrowth and plenty of beauty, and eventually found a good, wide track. Oh how wonderful that was! With the sun behind me I set off, even meeting some other people on the way. Soon there was a gate and four clear paths converged. By this time I wasn't keen to take the wrong one, so waited until a young couple pushing their baby came down the path I thought might well be the right one. They were curious about me and reassured me that they had come from the visitor centre. Where had I come from? We ended up talking about pilgrimage and being thankful for life, and they were really lovely. I thanked God for them as I walked on.

At the visitors centre I asked if they had a detailed map of the park, as my online OS map wasn't that helpful. Someone was summoned who could help, and although they didn't have a map, this man gave me wonderfully clear directions into Brentwood, bearing in mind my needs. It was marvellous to feel in control again. I bought an ice cream to celebrate!

The directions were easy to follow. He had even warned me about a difficult road crossing and suggested the best place to cross. Before long I came out of the park and beside a pond at Shenfield Green, where a man was standing in the water fishing. This, I thought, was quite strange, and I stopped to watch. A man came up to me having read my thoughts. "He's not really fishing", he explained. "We're dredging out all the stuff that gets chucked in!" So while his friend carried on dredging, we got into conversation about their finds, and also faith, pilgrimage, church and his own faith journey. A great honour it is to be a travelling friar sometimes!

As it was now late afternoon on a Sunday, there were no buses going out of Brentwood, so I decided to carry on walking down the roads and lanes of the 21 bus route, until the pavement stopped. My friend Eileen had said she would be waiting to come and fetch me from wherever I got to. The pavements continued all the way to the Brentwood Centre, after which they stopped abruptly. So I called Eileen and sat on the grass until she came and collected me. I could hardly walk by this time, so her kindness was much appreciated.

Eileen and Terry looked after me royally, with food and comfortable lodging, friendship and good conversation. We all sat and watched David Attenborough's new programme. It felt particularly pertinent viewing for this pilgrimage, challenging all of us on our life pilgrimage as we face the consequences of our human behaviour.

The other thing I learnt today is that when something seems impossible it's OK to ask for help. If we try to live so independently that we don't ask, we lose out on the loving kindness others give us as they help us. I'm not very good at asking for help – I never have been! I remember spending a whole double lesson trying to thread a needle once, rather than ask for help. Today showed me something about myself, and I'm grateful for that. Going on pilgrimage helps us to see what probably should have been obvious, but we've not recognised before. And this fresh understanding comes with the challenge to change course.

Day 3: Wyatt's Green to Chipping Ongar
Monday 14 September 2020

After breakfast, and talking through my route options, Eileen walked with me to the start of my walk. Today I would be walking all day, without any transport, unless I needed to change my plans. I was now in the Essex countryside, and although there were plenty of pretty lanes, I couldn't use them as there was nowhere to walk safely, lots of hidden bends, and no speed restrictions for traffic. There were also crowds of footpaths, but many of them were narrow and deeply rutted, with stiles, so I couldn't use these either! I decided to go for bridleways and pretend I was a horse.

It was another beautiful day, and I was travelling through a landscape of gentle hills, fields and wooded areas. I only met a few people on my way. Nearby was the village of Stondon Massey which I decided to visit, as our home while I was growing up was called Stondon Lodge. This was the choice of my Dad's Mum, Florence King, who loved this village and several of her relatives lived here. I'd never been here before, so this was a good opportunity to pay my respects. As I walked through the village I was imagining it as my Nanna Orme would have known it and so fondly remembered it. Obviously there is plenty of recent building, and the roads are busier, but it is a very pretty village, even now.

After the village I followed those tracks and bridlepaths to St Peter's Way, so called because the Way eventually leads to the ancient little church at Bradwell, where St Cedd arrived from Holy Island just off the Northumbrian coast to bring the Christian faith to the East Saxons.

He used the stones from a disused Roman fort to build the chapel, which is open every day of the year. This is probably possible because it contains nothing to steal, and is a fair distance from the village of Bradwell. Every July there is an ecumenical pilgrimage, and throughout the summer there is Sunday evening worship. Well worth a visit. The nearby Othona community can provide food and accommodation.

This is a poem I wrote for one of the annual pilgrimage festivals:

ST CEDD AND THE CURLEW'S CALL

East Saxons, I am on my way!
Your heart-cry came to call me here
Through weather foul and fair and clear
Through many a salt-stung, stormy day.

Came drifting north your need to find
God's blessing to enfold and keep
Your soul from fears and terrors deep
And rest your hearts in mercy kind.

And so from beach to waves and sky
The Spirit's breath to fill my sail,
I ride the sea through calm and gale
My prayers entwined with curlew's cry.

God is my witness that I pray
My boat shall beach upon your shore
And Gospel joy shall fill you more
And more with hope through every day.

So that, in future journeys here
Christ's people wend their joyful way
To celebrate and sing and pray,
Now full of hope and freed from fear!

After my stroke in 2012 it was to Bradwell that I yearned to go on a pilgrimage of thanksgiving, and as soon as I reckoned it was feasible (or probably a bit sooner) I did it. I used train, bus and taxi to the village of Bradwell and then tackled the two mile walk to the chapel. I had booked in at the Othona Community so I could be sure of a proper meal and accommodation, and as I staggered into the chapel I was very glad to have made that choice. Oh but how wonderful it was to be thanking God in this ancient, holy place! There would still be plenty more recovery, but here I knew that the first stage of recovery had been completed. St Peter's-on-the-Wall proved it!

So it was with all this in mind that I joined the St Peter's Way.

Although wide, the grass was very long and the track sloped sideways between hedgerow and ploughed field.

I needed frequent rests as my muscles sagged in protest at holding the walker level and encouraging it to negotiate long tussocks of grass. These rests were useful as I could stop and appreciate the birdsong, and check the map. There was a sharp right turn at some point and I didn't want to miss it.

When I found it, the narrow path went uphill, straight across a double field of dead cabbages. It had been on the news that the combination of Brexit and Covid had resulted in acres of vegetables dying instead of being picked. Now I was walking through the stinking evidence. The path was only wide enough for half my walker, so I varied my progress accordingly. My left side is weaker than my right, so I'd mainly have the left hand side on the path as I lifted the right side over the cabbages and up the hill. Whenever the strength in my right side gave out, I'd rest, listen to the swifts, and count up to fifteen as I swapped sides. Another rest, and then a count of ten persuading the walker up over cabbages on both sides while I walked in the middle. It was rather an exhausting journey, and seemed to be taking forever! I used this physical struggle as prayer for a fresh look at farming methods, with greater diversity, less fertiliser and more hedgerows. This huge wide field of dying cabbages was a kind of open air factory, which spelt out vulnerability.

When I finally reached the concrete path on the ridge, I sat and rested, drank some water and ate some nuts. I was still a long way from any roads and knew I needed to be careful. Once recovered I set off again. The route led through trees and over a couple of ditches, by narrow bridges not designed with my needs in mind. They took time, but were easier than the cabbage field.

One stile caused a few problems, but I cracked it by doing it in stages.

1) unload walker

2) push bags over stile

3) fold walker

4) push walker through a gap next to stile

5) carefully climb over stile

6) open walker and reload

It took ages, but that was fine. I felt really victorious as I stood on the new side of the stile having accomplished it!

When I emerged from the small wood there was a hill to climb, and in the distance I saw two people walking down. We greeted each other and they were a brother and sister out for a walk. How had I got over the stile, they wanted to know. The brother said there was another stile at the top of the hill, so they'd be happy to come with me and help. I protested that this would mean them going back the way they had already come. "That's fine" said the sister, "We're out for a walk, so it doesn't matter to us which way we go!" So we became friends as we all climbed the hill together, and I have to admit it was wonderful to have their help at the stile.

Such kindness today reminded me of the way I have been helped in my life pilgrimage by the willing kindness and help of others, who have been happy to put down their own plans for a while so as to be available for others. Sometimes I have been at the receiving end, and at other times I realise that I have been given the opportunity to walk back the way I have come so as to help another across a metaphorical stile. This brother and sister were an answer to my unspoken need, and I suppose we learn throughout our life pilgrimage, to recognise these opportunities for kindness which answer the needs of others.

Not only had I been helped physically. These people had also ministered to me emotionally and spiritually, cheering me up and spurring me on exactly when I needed their help! I went on my way rejoicing at the dappled light patterning the path, and feeling better equipped for whatever challenges lay ahead.

This next challenge came sooner than I expected. Fairly recently the farmland had been fenced off into paddocks for horses, and the new terrain didn't match up with those shown on my map. I tried several ways and could see where the footpath had previously gone, so decided my best route was to go down this little used and greatly overgrown route. At first it was just the kind of stop, start progress I was used to, but when it turned into an impassably narrow and overgrown path beside a strong fence, I didn't quite know what to do. I couldn't go forwards or backwards!

Just then a dog started barking near me, having heard my progress, so I called out to the dog. "Hello dog," I called, "is your owner near you by any chance? I think I need some help!" A woman looked out and saw me, then came across to the fence. "Mmm," she said, "it's going to be hard for you to get down there. The Council are supposed to keep it clear but they haven't managed to do that this year." And then she became an angel…

"If you can get over the fence," she said, "I'll take you through the farm to the lane if that would help?" So together we managed to get me over the fence, and we became friends as we walked together through her farm and out through the big gateway to the lane. It was wonderfully easy walking, and I felt very honoured. She was so kind and cheerful, it was a real pleasure to meet her.

Once on the lane I could find where I was on the map, and it wasn't far before a bridleway through trees led comfortably to the outskirts of High Ongar. A gentleman and his retriever walked with me past Nash Hall and the church to where the footpath continued west, crossing the stream by a splendidly wide bridge. A dog was enjoying a swim further along, as I turned up the hill before joining the path to the remains of a motte and bailey castle. Fingerprints of history remind us constantly of how our assumed permanence is in fact temporary.

I came out on to the A128 and walked into the centre of Chipping Ongar, where I found a fish and chip shop willing to sell me a large mug of tea. I sat outside to drink it, and then went down the Moreton Road to find my accommodation. Yet again the fine tuning of this final part of the day's walk included several wrong choices and I ended up asking directions until the door was opened and I was welcomed inside.

FAMILY RULES

1. Help each other and be thankful.
2. Know you are loved and pay with hugs and kisses.
3. Try new things, be happy and show compassion.
4. Be grateful, dream big and respect one another.

It was comfortable and had everything I needed, including the kind host and her son. For supper I went back to the chippy, and my host made some tea, so we shared time and stories as we ate. I thought back to the different people I had met during the day, and the help I had been given. And that reminded me of those we meet on our life pilgrimage – maybe for several years, or just a bus journey. Every conversation, every encounter, is a gift and an opportunity.

The other truth is that we have developed a very narrow, human view of time, based on our own average space between birth and death. This can result in an urgency to fit as much as possible into our human average timespan, rather than recognising that time is in fact multifaceted.

For instance, if instead we think with the timespan of a tree or a mountain, human scurrying within the universe is seen as a very short term activity. Today's reworking of how long it takes to cross a stile, for instance, or make a journey of ten miles, has helped me to view our life pilgrimage with a different time perspective. Earthed eternity within our human timeframe frees us up to live differently. Life is not about a linear time journey at all.

In God's economy, the present moment encapsulates all the past and future of which we are usually unaware. In God's eternal, inside/outside-time existence, all the different speeds of time exist together. The what and how are far more important than our 'are we nearly there yet?' way of living. This life pilgrimage of ours is not a race, but more a work of art.

Day 4: Chipping Ongar to Old Harlow
Tuesday 15 September 2020

After a good night's sleep I had breakfast and set off confidently on the route my host had advised. She did a lot of running and knew the area well. I was glad of her clear directions and descriptions. I would be using the Essex Way to Greensted church, then on through Epping Forest, crossing the M11, and maybe catching a bus from Epping to Harlow. I suppose in our life journey of faith this is how a spiritual mentor or guide can help us – having become familiar with the faith journey themselves they can help us on our way by useful advice and signs to look out for on our way.

It didn't take me long to reach the Essex Way. Some parts of this were level and easy going, while others were deeply rutted and overgrown. But I was becoming familiar with this and now found it quite acceptable – part of the proper way even though it was hard going. So often in life's journey we start to question whether we are on the right track, just because it happens to be hard work, and a struggle. An actual walk like this one reminds us that even through patches of nettles, or over deeply rutted and overgrown paths we are still on the right track. It just happens to be a tricky or uncomfortable part of the way. 'Right' doesn't necessarily equate with 'comfortable and easy'.

My attention was drawn to the diversity of plants in the hedgerows beside me. Hazel, hawthorn, dandelion, chickweed, elder, beech, apple, sloe, bramble…the whole creation sings of diversity and proclaims it. Strange, then, that our one human species within this diversity habitat, has managed to cheerfully destroy much of the diversity so as to make life more comfortable for us. And yet now we are finally realising that the delicate balance of diversity is vital, and extermination of species actually threatens the very survival of the exterminators.

Before long I came to the ancient wooden Greensted church, and spent some time praying there in the churchyard surrounded by peace and birdsong.

I remembered the pilgrimage we made here, completely organised and led by the youth group at St Margaret's in Leigh-on-Sea. We had slept the previous night in the church hall at Stock, and when we arrived here on Sunday afternoon we were joined by a good number of the congregation who had come in their cars. Together we worshipped. This church gives us a reminder that we are all part of a great pilgrim company, travelling through space and time, but always within the love of God. It was good to be here again.

The sun was hot as I walked on, and I was happy to see Epping Forest in the distance, with the promise of shade. On the way I stopped for lunch in a pub garden, choosing a shady table to sit at, and glad of the rest. Entering the forest, with its tall, wide canopy of leaves high above the forest floor was bliss, and I sat and drank some water as I drank in its loveliness. Perhaps some of Greensted church's wood came from trees growing then in this forest at Epping.

As I sat in its shade several people and their dogs saw me and stopped for a chat. I wasn't in a hurry and neither were they. Perhaps lockdown has taught us to slow down a bit. Some people wanted to know more about why I was here, and it felt both humbling, and an honour to be chatting the gospel in such a wise and attentive holy corner of God's creation.

I wondered how I was going to cross the M11, which I could hear increasingly as I walked through the forest. But my runner host had assured me the path to the bridge was clear, and there were no steps. Sure enough, through a break in the trees I

found the path leading up an incline to a footbridge high over the motorway. I could remember this being built, many years before, section by section, happy to find our regular trips to Coventry got gradually shorter. To my shame I don't think it occurred to me at the time that this huge gash through the forest had been a necessary part of the construction. I stood at the middle of the bridge to watch the traffic racing below, before crossing over to the next section of Epping Forest.

My map indicated that I was approaching the main road between Epping and Harlow, and showed a footpath running parallel to the road which looked more pleasant for walking, so I turned left. The track became increasingly narrow so I asked some walkers – a woman and her son – whether it led into Epping. They advised me not to take this route as recent building had made it harder to follow. They were also able to assure me that the road had a cycle track which I'd be able to walk on.

So I retraced my steps to the main path and followed it out to the road. By this time I was quite tired, and there was a bus stop, so I waited for the bus into Epping and then caught the Harlow bus from there. I was just in time for the school laden buses, so it was a noisy ride, and Harlow seemed to be in the middle of a roadworks spending spree. One passenger was getting more and more anxious as the bus was stopped again and again. I do hope he made it to his appointment on time.

The bus took us to Harlow central bus station, where I could find no information and no one to ask. Twice I was given wrong directions about which bus to take to Old Harlow, and where it left from. It was all rather confusing. But eventually I found the right stop, and a bus going the right way, so I climbed aboard, somewhat relieved. I knew I was to alight at the old post office, so watched every stop carefully. I saw no old post office and became suspicious when we seemed to be leaving Harlow behind. I should have checked earlier, of course.

I got off on a very busy road with nowhere safe for me to cross, and no idea where I was. Ok, I'll be honest, I started to cry a bit as I staggered along, willing my brain damaged body to keep going. I had reached the end of my strength, I think. But then I saw a young woman walking towards me and asked her how I could get to the old post office. She was kind and sympathetic, helped me over the road and told me there was no sign that the building I needed had once been a post office. That made me feel better, and less of an idiot. As I approached the bus stop a bus came, so I sensibly asked the driver to tell me when we were at the right stop.

She did, and I got off. I followed the map directions, but went wrong. A group of young people set me right, as a new road layout had changed things. The road I needed now came to a dead end before the main road, but I found a pedestrian path, asked again for directions (I was a bit paranoid now about making any more mistakes as I knew I was flagging) and they said the house I was looking for was next but one! I could have hugged them!

But I wasn't quite there yet. There were instructions for getting in, which my tired brain took a couple of goes to decipher, and once inside, more instructions and a flight of stairs with no lift.

Looking up at them, they seemed like a mountain. So I found somewhere downstairs to leave my walker, and climbed those stairs with my luggage, like a dog. At the top I found my room, with a key in the door. It was comfortable and airy, with a good view, and I lay on the bed, exhausted. But I had made it, and I was happy!

After a doze I had a shower, changed, and explored downstairs. I found a large well equipped kitchen, pleasant living room, laundry room and garden, and also four or five other residents who showed me where everything was. Some were students, others were staying here while on business in the area. One was working on the Cross Rail construction. Another was a geologist, checking out the ground where a large building is going to be built. It was a happy overnight stop, with plenty of laughter and conversation, good company and all the facilities I could wish for, all included in the price. I slept very well.

As I thought back over the day, which had included frustrations as well as relief, and exhaustion as well as refreshment, I could see how my week long journey modelled my life journey. That mixture of the easy and difficult, of frustration and relief, of confusion and certainty, it's all normal! Stuff happens. I wonder if we are fed the lie that 'normal' is the easy, the relief, the certainty and so on. Once we buy into this untruth, disappointment and a sense of failure loom large whenever the true normal kicks in. Do we need to recognise the lie for what it is, and learn to live within the true normal, where both ups and downs are simply part of the pattern?

Day 5: Old Harlow to Cheshunt
Wednesday 16 September 2020

Next morning I had breakfast, packed up my washed clothes, and set off. My walking wasn't great after getting overtired the previous day, so I didn't rush to get going. I tried to do my body the courtesy of listening to it! I first walked over the road to the church I could see from my bedroom, then walked on pavements down to the river Stort. It was actually rather nice to be walking past houses and gardens along pavements designed for pedestrians for a change. I could see why town councils had introduced this communal infrastructure. It certainly made life easier!

Beside the waterway was a firmly constructed towpath which was clearly well used by walkers, dogs and their owners, joggers and cyclists. It was quite busy. There were even mobility scooters, though I didn't see any others with walking aids. Surely I wasn't the only person who wanted to continue walking, even if it was less straightforward? I wondered if I would start a walking club for walkers with wheels when I got home? We could take our time and walk along by the sea, stopping somewhere for coffee!

At one point on the river a boat was heading for the lock I'd just passed, so I went back to watch what happened. The strong lock gates held shut as the pressure of water increased, and the water level rose, lifting the boat to the same level as the next section of the river. And the boat's dog wagged his tail at the rising water. A bit of local drama witnessed and photographed by quite a crowd of us, and no doubt posted on social media around the world!

By one houseboat was a bench with a carved invitation to take a break and enjoy the peace. Seeing this tempting invitation I put the brakes on my walker and sat on the bench. Time for some water and a snack! As I left I saw on shadow move on the houseboat, so called out my thanks, and received a waved reply.

Sometimes I'd be overtaken (unsurprisingly) and then later find the overtakers sitting in the sun so I became the overtaker, and we'd all laugh at the turn of events. Sometimes the towpath left the river for a while before rejoining it further on.

Further on I met some people who recognised my clerical collar and we chatted about their church and my pilgrimage. When I reached the attractive village of Roydon I had an excellent pub meal in their sunny garden, then went into the village church which was open and welcoming, and carefully laid out so as to make prayer a natural and less scary activity.

I sat in the peace and prayed with great thankfulness for the precious and fragile gift of life. Another conversation, and an invitation to join them again whenever possible.

From Roydon village I walked to the train station, and caught the train from here to Cheshunt, via Broxbourne beside the river Lea. By the time I reached Cheshunt the day was very warm again as I made my way to the centre of the town. I could see on the map that I was now skirting London, just north of the M25, and would need to cross the A10 to get to my lodgings for the night. It looked as if there was a footbridge but I rather dreaded any steps!

I found the footbridge and yes, there were lots of steps, but no other way of crossing the road. So I bought a drink and snack from a small but well stocked Asian shop, and demolished these as I rested before tackling the bridge. By now I was not feeling fazed by the challenge, but was getting more used to seeing challenges as both normal and also as learning opportunities!

Helpfully the steps were widely enough spaced to make it possible without resorting to the dog method, and of course there was that flat path across the top before the descent, when I had gravity on my side. I was now into the close area of my target, but as I expected, this was often the hardest to work out. Often there were no numbers on the houses, and even google maps would prove inadequate for the task. I found the actual road easily enough, and walked down and up it without success. Soon someone walked down the road who I could ask, but they had no idea either.

Eventually however, I asked someone who knew, and as the sun was setting and no one answered the door, I sat in the low sun, wearing my waterproof against the chill of Autumn. This was the only occasion I needed my coat. After an hour I tried the door again, and phoned my host. I had the impression that he had forgotten I was coming, as he was still at work in London, and very apologetic and polite. Human error happens sometimes. Been there. Done that.

The sun had now set, and I was getting cold as I waited. I knew this would do me no good, so I set off back the way I'd come, till I came to the A10. I didn't have enough energy to face the bridge, but was happy to see an open pub, The Green Man, where I was welcomed in, directed to a comfortable seat next to a log fire, and brought a pot of tea and some toast. How lovely was that! I was able to warm up and crank up the energy levels before going back to the house to which I now knew the way. My host and his sister were kind and helpful, so I ended up with yet another positive experience and an excellent sleep.

Day 6: Cheshunt to Hertford
Thursday 17 September 2020

My host's sister and I shared breakfast before I left Cheshunt and the constant Nigerian radio evangelists, and set off along Silver Street and down the Chain Walk.

It felt so good to be out in the countryside again, and I reflected on those familiar times on our life pilgrimage when our natural forgetfulness or mistakes can inadvertently cause problems for others. We may not even be aware of the troubles we cause. (I remember a wordless picture book my children and I enjoyed, called *Rosie's Walk*. Rosie the hen had no idea of the chaos she caused, and it was funny for us to see what Rosie never noticed!)

And yet there is also an opportunity given for blessing through our muddles and mistakes, as for instance the staff at The Green Man could see my need and responded so wholeheartedly. Maybe our human calling is to mop up any spillages we encounter!

There was still warmth in the sun today, and my route took me through some stables, with glossy horses staring curiously at me, and tracks that would have been walked by many before the advent of cars and trains. I saw the fine Northaw and Cuffley viaduct before reaching Cuffley, where I stopped for coffee before catching the train to Hertford North station. The station staff at Cuffley were really helpful. They enabled me to get up the steps on to the platform, helped me aboard with a ramp, and phoned ahead to the staff at Hertford, so I benefited from assisted travel even without booking it. British railways at its best! I enjoyed the two-station ride, with lovely scenery to look out at.

I had taken the train because my body was tiring, but also I would have more time to spend in Hertford, which is such an interesting city. There is plenty of history, and I was able to look round the museum, as well as the castle ruins and park, the complex rivers Beane and Rib, and wander through the centre, and King's Meads. It was like having a free day, even though I was still doing a fair bit of walking.

From King's Meads there is quite a steep path up through the trees which brought me out to a high vantage point and an ancient church. From here I could look over this city, which I really hope to revisit one day.

For today, I carried on uphill to the district of Bengeo, where I had booked to stay the night. On the way was an open church, welcoming people to come in for private prayer. I went in and felt enveloped by God's loving presence.

The vicar dashed in on his way to close the church before collecting his children from school, but he was so willing to let

me stay awhile and insisted he could collect the children first
and close the church later. So kind. I could see from the
newsletter and the website that this church community was
actively working, and prayed for their continuing ministry
before I left.

Bengeo seemed to be at the top of a hill, and I found the house
I was looking for quite easily as it was numbered and fitted the
description. My host and her mother were in and welcomed me
into their lovely home. They also invited me to share their

evening meal, and they knew the church I had found. I much enjoyed their company, and thanked God for their hospitality. We wouldn't appreciate the ups in life if there weren't a few downs as well!

That evening Christians Aware was holding a zoomed meeting, with bishop John Perumbalath speaking, and thanks to the internet I was able to lie in bed and join the meeting.

During the night I woke up and drew back the curtains. The sky was crammed with stars! I think that, being on a hill, Bengeo was a dark place, where stars could be seen in all their stunning beauty. It reminded me of when I was living in the Peak District at Buxton, and walked the lanes around local villages staring up at the huge number of stars. Sadly we blot out this sight too often, and maybe that makes us forget that we are part of the vast universe.

I felt I had made friendships here in Hertford, and promised myself I would return some time.

Day 7: Hertford to Hatfield
Friday 18 September 2020

Next morning I had breakfast and felt quite sad, not only to be leaving Hertford, but also to be nearing the end of my pilgrimage. There is something wonderfully liberating about being nomadic, travelling in God's company and without any other agenda. Was this pilgrimage simply an escape from real life? I hoped it was more than this.

Once again I would be using public transport at first, so as to have more time to walk at Hatfield. Also I was aware of how my walking wasn't great, and I didn't want to overdo it. So it was by bus that I travelled, via Welwyn Garden City, and there was plenty to see on my way, and fellow passengers to talk with as we waited for the bus together outside Hertford North station.

From Hatfield bus station I first worked out how I would later make my way to my night stay, and then I walked through Old Hatfield to Hatfield House, which I had never visited before. It felt extra poignant to be walking through the historical events and famous lives as my own pilgrimage spanned both space and time. I walked all round the grounds – the detailed formal gardens and the areas of woodland and paths, landscaped lakes and wide views. Here the young Queen Elizabeth I would have walked, as events played out around her. She was only three when her mother was beheaded.

For each of us too there is a context within which our life journey is played out. Sometimes I have wondered if I was born 'for such a time as this', but actually I think we all are. You and I are the only ones who can act for good within our own time frame. Opportunities for being people of blessing abound, if only we are not too preoccupied to notice. Maybe our commission is to live attentively during our short lifespan, so that through lives well lived the world may be blessed, healed and encouraged. However old or young we are, however able bodied or mentally balanced, this commission stays viable, I reckon, and attentiveness is the key. I've been surprised on this pilgrimage how often blessing to others has only happened when I'm unable to do something for myself, and need to ask others for help. I suppose St Francis would think of this as a kind of blessed poverty.

It took me quite a while to negotiate crossings over and under roundabouts and busy roads, on my way across Hatfield, and I was glad of the trusty OS maps on my phone. The house was in a residential area on the west side of the town, and I had chosen to stay here because it looked closest to the path I would be taking on my final walk into St Alban's. Clear instructions had been texted to me by my host, so I found it easily, walked round the back as directed and was greeted by a full size replica of Michelangelo's David in the back garden! That cheered me as it gave me some idea of what kind of crazy, creative person might be my host.

Sure enough, Neil had a houseful of interesting people, and clearly loved being the perfect host. This was the perfect place for me to find as I approached the last day of my pilgrimage. Excellent company, generously shared food, and even wine. I soon felt one of the household community, and had a good night's sleep.

Day 8: Hatfield to St Albans
Saturday 19 September 2020

So this was it. I prayed and dressed carefully, had breakfast and set off. The disused railway line was right behind the house, so I only had a short walk down the street to find it. It was smooth, wide and lined with trees, easy and interesting walking.

Soon I came across a station which had been painstakingly and lovingly restored. Apparently one cycling commuter had been saddened by the state it was in, wishing someone would do something about it. One day it occurred to him that he might be that someone! Each day he stopped to clear a bit more, and soon others joined him, caught his vision and together they turned it into the magical ghost station it is now. What a story!

It matches the story of how St Francis restored the broken down church of San Damiano, but it also echoes what this book and this pilgrimage are about, and I am discovering.

Each of us, on our life pilgrimage, are the someone, needed to do something about whatever and whoever needs healing, clearing, restoring and refreshing. I have met so many wonderful people doing exactly that on this walk, all different, and all doing what they can, not what they can't. They do this with their varied personalities and as part of their own journeys of faith. All their past experience, with both painful and happy memories, is shaping them into those who can do what God needs doing, whether they know God by name or not.

To be part of this vast life pilgrimage of ours, in space and time, is an incredible honour, and yes, I am so very thankful for this privilege of being alive.

As I got closer to the city I had a text telling me that my niece Jane was on her way to meet me, and soon after I saw her in the distance.

It was very lovely to walk those last miles together. We could see the abbey from the path, and made our way to it. Journey's end.

Outside on the grassy hill were both my lovely daughters and their families there to welcome me, and I have to say that although the journey of a pilgrimage is as important as the destination, there is also an extraordinary joy inside you as the journeying is accomplished. Arrival is the fulfilment of the journey.

And in our life pilgrimage?

I wonder if we have sometimes lost sight of death being destination, and heavenly welcome being something of a joyful healing and fulfilment. Not that we have done everything right, or made use of each and every opportunity, but that God's love and forgiveness has enabled us, taught us, and believed in us every step of the way.

I was welcomed by the dean, Jeffrey John, and given a guided tour of the cathedral by Alan. It was good to pray at the tombs of both Alban and the priest whose Christian example converted him. Such a short time he had before facing the challenge of either renouncing his new Christian faith or being killed.

How would we respond to that challenge, I wondered?

The priest, too, though enabled by Alban to escape, was later caught and killed. So at Saint Alban's Cathedral both these faithful, steadfast and courageous martyrs have been laid to rest, and great numbers of pilgrims have been inspired by their example and cheered on their own faith journey.

My guide, Paul, took me to a café later, once my family had left, for a much-needed cup of tea. And he accompanied me to my lodging for the night so I didn't even need to work out how to get there. Another lovely welcome from my host and her son, and a comfortable room. When I explained I would be going to the cathedral on Sunday morning she said she would be going as well, so we could go together!

That evening I walked down to an M&S for some supper, and slept well.

Day 9: St Albans
Sunday 20 September 2020

After breakfast my host and I walked to the cathedral, which was open again after the first lockdown, but with social distancing in place. There was even a choir.

They welcomed me publicly and thanked me for my books, which they had used. The dean preached about how we don't always take kindly to the wideness of God's love, as we would often prefer love to be on our own, decidedly narrower terms.

I agree, and have so often noticed that tendency in my own life pilgrimage!

Afterwards I was treated to coffee, shown the amazing ancient frescoes, and driven to the station by someone who remembered me leading a retreat they were on. I felt entirely surrounded by friends. I would be travelling to my Walthamstow family for a day or so, rather than going straight home. I needed a bit of time for adjustment.

EPILOGUE

I'd like to end this story with a blessing for all of you who are engaged with your own life pilgrimage at the moment. Maybe you are just starting out, or have recently discovered a God-given nudge. Maybe some of your past life experiences continue to haunt your present reality, or there has been damage caused to you that requires the healing only the Maker can give.

I don't know you personally, probably, but God our Maker does know you well, and holds you in deep affection. By God you are believed in and are completely acceptable. God knows what would really make you happy and at peace in yourself.

- ❖ So step out into the rest of your days, however few or many that may be.

- ❖ Step out curiously, bravely, attentively, ready to learn and willing to be changed.

- ❖ Let God's values refresh yours.

- ❖ Allow God's attitudes to shift or enlarge your own.

- ❖ Each morning be thankful before you get up.

- ❖ Remember how privileged you are to be alive, and choose to live the day as well as you can.

- ❖ You may not match up to your understanding of what this means, but that's OK. Before you sleep, make peace with your Maker and commit yourself to God's care.

- ❖ Live each of your days as if it is your last, and one of those days you'll be right!

Above all, may your life pilgrimage, given to you as a gift, be such a blessing to the time and space you inhabit, that your life will have helped and healed the good Earth and all its inhabitants, animal, vegetable and mineral.

And to God be the glory! Amen.

RESOURCES I HAVE FOUND HELPFUL ON MY LIFE PILGRIMAGE

LIFE! (People and places)

Adam, David, his books on Celtic spirituality

Anon, *The Cloud of Unknowing*

Attenborough, David, all series!

Augustine of Hippo, *Confessions*

Brother Andrew, *God's Smuggler*

Bunyan, John, *Pilgrim's Progress*

Cox, Brian, *The Planets* and other Science series

Dr Who series on BBC i-player

Harry Potter books and films

Hughes, Gerard W., *Walk To Jerusalem: In Search Of Peace*

Lewis, C.S., *Surprised by Joy*

Magnusson, Sally, *The Sealwoman's Gift*

Muggeridge, Malcolm, *Jesus Rediscovered*

Ten Boom, Corrie, *The Hiding Place*

Vanstone, W.H., *Love's Endeavour, Love's Expense*

Films: *Shawshank Redemption, Finding St Francis (TSSF),*
      Cry Freedom, Long Walk to Freedom,
      The Mission, Gandhi

Printed in Great Britain
by Amazon

46900504R10115